ENGLISH
GRAMMAR

ENGLISH
GRAMMAR

John Shepheard

TEACH YOURSELF BOOKS

With thanks to Jane and Luke

For UK order queries: please contact Bookpoint Ltd, 39 Milton Park, Abingdon, Oxon
OX14 4TD. Telephone: (44) 01235 400414, Fax: (44) 01235 400454. Lines are open from
9.00–6.00, Monday to Saturday, with a 24 hour message answering service.
Email address: orders@bookpoint.co.uk

For U.S.A. & Canada order queries: please contact NTC/Contemporary Publishing,
4255 West Touhy Avenue, Lincolnwood, Illinois 60646 – 1975, U.S.A.
Telephone: (847) 679 5500, Fax: (847) 679 2494.

Long renowned as the authoritative source for self-guided learning – with more than
30 million copies sold worldwide – the *Teach Yourself* series includes over 200 titles in
the fields of languages, crafts, hobbies, sports, and other leisure activities.

British Library Cataloguing in Publication Data
A catalogue entry for this title is available from The British Library.

Library of Congress Catalog Card Number: on file

First published in UK 2001 by Hodder Headline Plc, 338 Euston Road, London, NW1 3BH.

First published in US 2001 by NTC/Contemporary Publishing, 4255 West Touhy Avenue,
Lincolnwood (Chicago), Illinois 60646 – 1975 U.S.A.

The 'Teach Yourself' name and logo are registered trade marks of Hodder & Stoughton Ltd.

Copyright © 2001 John Shepheard

Typeset by Transet Limited, Coventry, England.
Printed in Great Britain for Hodder & Stoughton Educational, a division of Hodder
Headline Plc, 338 Euston Road, London NW1 3BH by Cox & Wyman Ltd, Reading,
Berkshire.

Impression number   10 9 8 7 6 5 4 3 2 1
Year   2005 2004 2003 2002 2001

CONTENTS

Modal verbs

INTRODUCTION

Instruction words

In English   **In your language**

Meaning   _____

Form   _____

Match   _____

Practice   _____

Write   _____

Check the answers   _____

For example   _____

Meaning

♥ = 1

♥♥ = 2

♥♥♥ = 3

♥♥♥♥ = 4

Form

1 = one
2 = two
3 = three
4 = four

Match **the numbers to the words.**

a 1
b 2
c 3
d 4

four
three
one
two

✓ Check the answers

(They are at the back of the book.)

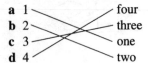

a 1
b 2
c 3
d 4

four
three
one
two

Practice

Write **the numbers.**

1   *one*
2 _____
3 _____
4 _____

✓ Check the answers

1 *one*
2 *two*
3 *three*
4 *four*

Grammar Words

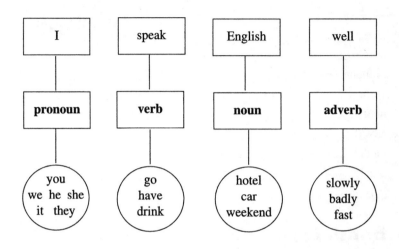

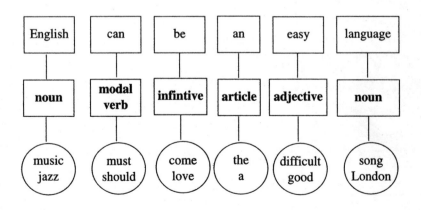

In English	In your language

pronoun	_____
verb	_____
noun	_____
adverb	_____
modal verb	_____
article	_____
adjective	_____

British English/American English

For example: I live in a [flat/apartment] in Hong Kong.

Flat is British English.
Apartment is American English.

For example: [Can/May] I help you?

Can I help you? is British English.
May I help you? is American English.

1 | *Present Simple*
am/is/are – be (positive)
■ I'm from the USA
■ It's famous
■ They're Australian

Meaning

1 Match the sentences to the pictures.

a   **You're** in room 3, the elementary class.

b   **I'm** from the U.S.A. My **name's** Doug.

c   **We're** 33 years old.

d   **It's** famous and **it's** in New York.

e   **They're** Australian.

f   **She's** Australian.

g   **He's** hungry.

✓ **Check the answers**

Form

2 Complete the table with the verbs in the box below.

	's	'm	're

I	**a** *'m*	
He She It	**b** _____	in New York.
We You They	**c** _____	

✓ **Check the answers**

3 *'m*, *'s*, *'re* are short forms or *contractions*. Use contractions in speaking and informal writing. Match the long forms in the box, with the *contractions*.

	are	am	is

a	I'm	→	I	*am*
b	She's	→	She	_____
c	He's	→	He	_____
d	It's	→	It	_____
e	We're	→	We	_____
f	You're	→	You	_____
g	They're	→	They	_____

✓ **Check the answers**

Practice

4 Circle ◯ the correct verb.

a 80% of animals is/am/are insects.
b Tomatoes am/is/are fruits.

c The body am/are/is 90% water.

d The elephant am/is/are the only animal with four knees.

e Number 13 is/am/are unlucky in many cultures.

f It is/are/am lucky in Italy.

g 'I 's/'re/'m a Berliner.' (*US President, John F Kennedy in Berlin in 1960*)

h 'You am/is/are the sunshine of my life.' (*Stevie Wonder*)

i 'We 're/'m/'s more popular than Jesus now.' (*John Lennon about the Beatles in 1965*)

j 'She are/am/is in fashion.' (*Suede from 'Head Music'*)

k 'He 's/'m/'re a real nowhere man...' (*Beatles song 'Nowhere Man'*)

l 'The future 'm/'s/'re black.' (*James Baldwin*).

✓ **Check the answers**

⚠ Common mistakes

5 Find the mistakes and correct them.

a He're English.   *He's English.*

b Her name Emma.   _____

c They from New York.   _____

d My car it's very new.   _____

e You is a teacher.   _____

f I Japanese.   _____

g She a very good teacher. _____

h We from Tokyo.   _____

✓ **Check the answers**

Now you

Write about you and your family and friends.

I		a student
My brother		married
My sister		12 years old
My mother	am/'m	from Poland
My father	is/'s	young
My parents	are/'re	old
My friends		beautiful…
My best friend		

_____

_____

_____

_____

➤ Unit 2 *am/is/are – be* (questions and negative)

2 Present Simple am/is/are – be (questions and negative)

- Am I in the photo?
- Is she your mother?
- They aren't my brothers

Meaning

Emma's Photographs

Emma with her photographs and a friend, Samantha.

1 Match the photographs to the dialogues.

i	**Samantha**	Emma, **are you** in front of the elephant?
	Emma	No, **I'm not** in front of the elephant. Look – I'm on the horse.
ii	**Samantha**	**Am I** in the photo with the bus?
	Emma	No, **you're not**! That's me.
iii	**Samantha**	Look at the two boys with the dog. **Are they** your brothers?
	Emma	No – **they aren't** my brothers. They're the [neighbours/neighbors].
iv	**Samantha**	**Is she** your mother?
	Emma	No, **she isn't** my mother – she's my aunt.
	Samantha	And the man with her – **is he** your uncle?
	Emma	No, **he isn't** my uncle – he's my father!
v	**Samantha**	**Is it** in Paris?
	Emma	No, **it isn't** Paris. **It's** in London – **it's** the Crystal Palace BBC TV Tower.
vi	**Samantha**	**Are we** in that photograph? There on the right.
	Emma	Yes, but **we aren't** on the right. Look, we're at the back.

✔ Check the answers

Form

Questions

2 Complete the table with the words in the box.

~~he~~	am	it	are

a _____	I	
Is	**b** *he* she **c** _____ Emma	in the photograph?
d _____	we you they	

Negative

3 Complete the table with the words in the box.

isn't	not	aren't	'm

I	**a** _____	**b** _____	
He She It Emma	**c** _____		in the photograph.
We You They	**d** _____		

Negative short form

4 Complete the sentence.

isn't is short for _____

✔ Check the answers

⚠ Common mistakes

5 Correct the mistakes in the questions and negative sentences.

a I amn't from Iceland.   *I'm not from Iceland.*
b You are German?   _____
c They not happy.   _____
d She not is short.   _____
e He your boyfriend?   _____
f I aren't in the photograph.   _____
g We no are happy.   _____
h You no French.   _____

 Check the answers

Practice

6 Write true sentences – positive or negative.

a Paris / the capital of Germany	*Paris isn't the capital of Germany.*
b I / hungry	_____
c Luxembourg / a big country	_____
d London / in France	_____
e Gold / cheap	_____
f Boxing / dangerous	_____
g Oranges / vegetables	_____
h I / Irish	_____
i Potatoes / vegetables	_____
j We / from Mars	_____
k Charles / the king of England	_____
l Al Gore / the U.S. president	_____

✓ **Check the answers**

7 Two reporters arrive in a hotel. They go to interview Pierre, a writer. Write questions with the words in brackets.

Reporter 1 a   *Are we late*   ? (late)
Reporter 2 No, we aren't.
Reporter 1 b _____? (at the right hotel)
Reporter 2 Yes, we are.
Reporter 1 Hello, Pierre. We're here to interview you.
      c _____? (French)
Pierre   No, I'm not.
Reporter 1 d _____? (Swiss)
Pierre   Yes, I am.
Reporter 1 e _____? (French your first language)
Pierre   Yes, it is.
Reporter 1 f _____? (it your cat in the photograph)
Pierre   Yes, it is.
Reporter 1 g _____? (your wife Swiss)
Pierre   No, she isn't.
Reporter 1 h _____? (she French)
Pierre   Yes, she is.
Reporter 1 i _____? (they your children)
Pierre   Yes, they are.

Reporter 1 j _____? (they twins)
Pierre   No, they aren't.

✓ **Check the answers**

8 Complete the sentences. Use the short answers in exercise 7 to help you.

Are you French?   **a** Yes, I *am*
                          b No, I _____

Am I late?   Yes, you *are*
                          No, you *aren't*

Is she your wife?   **c** Yes, _____
                          d No, _____

Is he Swiss?   Yes, he *is*
                          No, he *isn't*

Is it your cat?   **e** Yes, _____
                          f No, _____

Are we late?   **g** Yes, _____
                          h No, _____

Are they twins?   **i** Yes, _____
                          j No, _____

✓ **Check the answers**

9 Give true short answers to the questions.

a Is New York in the U.S.A.?   *Yes, it is.*
b Is Berlin in Switzerland?   _____
c Are you Welsh?   _____
d Are you a student of English?   _____
e Is President Kennedy alive?   _____
f Is Princess Diana alive?   _____
g Are the Alps in Switzerland?   _____
h Are apples vegetables?   _____
i Is the author of this book an English
   speaker?   _____
j Is the author of this book a man?   _____
k Are we at the end of exercise 10?   _____

l   Are we at the end of exercise 9?   _____

✓ **Check the answers**

Now you

Write negative sentences about you and your family.

a   Write one thing true about all of you.
    We _____

b   Write one thing about you.
    I _____

c   Write one thing about your mother, father, sister or brother.
    He/she _____

> Unit 1 *am/is/are* (positive)
> Unit 14 *was/were* (positive and negative)

3 Present Simple there is/there are (positive and negative)

- There is(n't) a problem
- There are(n't) 44 letters

Meaning

1 Find the answers to the questions in the text below.

a The pronunciation of the letter 'a' in 'apple' and 'any' is the same. True or False?

b The pronunciation of the letter 'p' in 'park' and 'cup' is the same. True or False?

A – Z?

There are 44 sounds in English but **there aren't** 44 letters in the English alphabet. English has only 26 letters in the alphabet. So **there is** a big problem here!

There's only one way to say the letter 'p', but **there isn't** only one way to say the letter 'a'. In fact, **there are** six ways to say the letter 'a'. In the words: apple, army, able, about, all, any – we say the 'a' in a different way!

 Check the answers

Form

2 Answer the questions about *there is/there are*. Do we:

a use **there is** with singular nouns or plural nouns?

b use **there are** with singular nouns or plural nouns?

 Check the answers

3 Complete the tables with the words in the box. Use the text on page 11 to help you.

are	aren't	~~is~~	is	isn't

Positive

There	**a** *is* 's	a problem
	b ___	problems

Negative

There	**c** ____ not **d** _____	a problem
	are not **e** ____	44 letters

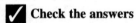 Check the answers

⚠ Common mistakes

4 Correct the mistakes.

a It is a book on the table.
   There is a book on the table.

b No are volcanoes in England.
   _____

c There is palm trees in Los Angeles.
   _____

d It is a car in the street.
   _____

✓ Check the answers

Practice

5 Write true sentences with *there is* or *there are*. Use the words below.

months	sun	days	vowel	days

a 12 / in a year

   There are 12 months in a year

b 1 / in the word 'March'

   _____

c 7 / in a week

   _____

d 30 / in April

   _____

e 1 / in the solar system

   _____

✓ **Check the answers**

Now you

Write three sentences about where you live. You can use the words below.

hospital   [cinema(s)/movie theater(s)]   hotel(s)   university
[sports centre/fitness center]

a *There's* _____
b *There isn't* _____
c *There are* _____

➤ Unit 4 *is there?/are there?* (questions)
➤ Unit 15 *there was/there were*

4

Present Simple
Is there?/Are there? (questions)

■ Is there an opera house in Sydney?
■ Are there elephants in India?

Meaning

1 Match the questions with the true answers.

> ### Quiz
>
> **a** Is there an opera house in Sydney, Australia?   No, there aren't.
> **b** Are there lakes in Saudi Arabia?   Yes, there is.
> **c** Are there elephants in India?   No, there isn't.
> **d** Is there a [metro/subway] in Oxford?   Yes, there are.

✓ **Check the answers**

Form

2 Answer the questions about *there is/there are*.

a Use *is there?* with singular nouns. True or False?
b Use *are there?* with plural nouns. True or False?

✓ **Check the answers**

3 Complete the table. Use the text of the quiz to help you.

are	are	~~is~~	there	there	isn't	aren't

a *Is*	there	a lake there?	Yes, **c** _____ is No, there **d** _____
b _____	there	lakes there?	Yes, there **e** _____ No, **f** _____ **g** _____

✓ **Check the answers**

Common mistakes

4 Correct the mistakes.

a Are people on the moon?
   Are there people on the moon?

b No, they aren't.

_____

c Is an American flag on the moon?

_____

d Yes, it is.

_____

✓ Check the answers

Practice

5 It's time to make dinner. Write four questions about what is in the fridge. Use the words in the boxes. Use each word only once.

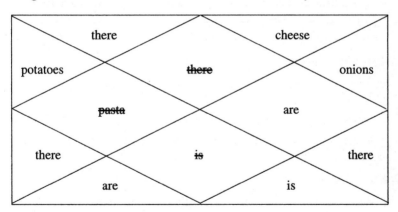

a   *Is there pasta in the fridge?*
b _____?
c _____?
d _____?

6 Put the words in the correct order to make questions about transport in London or New York.

a bus/there/airport/to/is/a/the?
   Is there a bus to the airport?

b trains/after midnight/there/are?

_____

c tickets/cheap/are/[at/on] weekends/there?

_____

d are/taxis/there/Central Station/outside?

_____

 Check the answers

Now you

Write two questions about Perth, Australia using *is there?* and *are there?*

a _____

b _____

➤ Unit 3 *there is/there are* (positive and negative)
➤ Unit 15 *there was/there were*

5 | *Present Simple* full verbs (positive and negative)

- I work
- I don't work
- She works
- She doesn't work

Meaning

Corrie Richards is 45 years old. She lives in England. Answer the questions from the text.

1 Corrie is in **a** a hotel?

              b a school?

              c a prison?

I **wake up** at 6:45 P.M. and first I **go** to the [toilet/bathroom]. Then I **get** hot water, **make** coffee, **smoke** a cigarette, **listen** to a little music and **write**. I **think** – why prison at my age? At 8 A.M. the doors **open** and the siren **sounds**. Another day **begins**. I **talk** with the girls, **take** a shower and **start** work. I **don't have** breakfast, as I **work** in the kitchens and I **eat** the food there. The work **pays** for my telephone calls. I **phone** my children in Holland. They **don't visit** me – it's too expensive. The work **doesn't pay** for cigarettes or the TV in my room. My mother **sends** me money for them.

✓ **Check the answer**

2 The verbs in **bold** are in the *Present Simple*. Answer the question: the *Present Simple* here is for (a) routines and habits or (b) actions we see now?

✓ **Check the answer**

Form

3 Look at the verbs in the text and complete the table with *work*, *pays*, *don't*, or *doesn't*.

Present Simple

Positive		**Negative**	
I We You **a** *work.* They My children		I We You **b** _____ visit. They My children	
He She It **c** _____ . The work		He She It **d** _____ pay. The work	

don't is short for **do not**
doesn't is short for **does not**

 Check the answers

Tip

Learn the lines:

She love*S* me
She doe*S*n't love me
She love*S* me
She doe*S*n't love me

Only **one** third person *S* in the negative.

⚠ Mistakes with the negative

4 Put ☑ for a correct sentence and ☒ for an incorrect sentence.

a	She doesn't works.	☒	**j**	They don't phone her.	☐
b	She works.	☑	**k**	I eat not breakfast.	☐
c	Corrie no works.	☐	**l**	I don't eat breakfast.	☐
d	Corrie doesn't work.	☐	**m**	You not smoke.	☐
e	He don't visit Corrie.	☐	**n**	You don't smoke.	☐
f	He doesn't visit Corrie.	☐	**o**	We do n't send money.	☐
g	I not wake up at 6:45 A.M.	☐	**p**	We don't send money.	☐
h	I don't wake up at 6:45 A.M.	☐	**q**	The money does not pay for TV.	☐
i	They doesn't phone her.	☐	**r**	The money not pays for TV.	☐

Practice

5 Make true sentences.

People		close its eyes
Kangaroos		jump
Elephants	don't	go around the earth
A snake	doesn't	bite
A male mosquito		live on Mars
The sun		walk backwards

a People *don't* *live on Mars.*

b Kangaroos _____

c Elephants _____

d A snake _____

e A male mosquito _____

f The sun _____

6 Mr. Jones is at the police station after a fire in his [neighbours'/ neighbors'] house. The policeman wants information. Mr. Jones is very nervous. Complete his answers. They are all negative.

Police	So, you smoke, Mr. Jones.
Mr. Jones	**a** No, I *don't smoke*.
Police	But your wife smokes...
Mr. Jones	**b** No, she _____ _____.

Police	Very well. Your two sons smoke, Mr. Jones.
Mr. Jones	**c** No, they _____ _____.
Police	I see. Now, you and your wife see your neighbours quite often.
Mr. Jones	**d** No, we _____ _____ them very often.
Police	I understand the problem here, Mr. Jones.
Mr. Jones	**e** No, you _____ _____ the problem at all.

7 Complete the true sentences with the verb in the correct form. Some are positive and some are negative. Use the verbs in the box only once.

tell   eat   rises   ~~go~~   work   grow   believe   live

a The earth *goes* around the sun.
b We're vegetarians. We _____ meat.
c Liars _____ the truth.
d Rice _____ in cold countries.
e The sun _____ in the east.
f A cashier _____ in a supermarket.
g I'm an atheist. I _____ in God.
h You're from California. You _____ on the Atlantic Ocean.

✓ **Check the answers**

Now you

Write about your habits or routines.

a *I* _____
b *I don't* _____
c *I* _____

Write about your friend's or brother's or sister's or partner's routines or habits.

d *S/he* _____
e *S/he doesn't* _____
f _____

> Unit 6 *Present Simple* third person singular (positive)
> Unit 7 *Present Simple* (questions)

6 | *Present Simple* full verbs – third person singular (positive)
- He works
- She works

Meaning

Sumo wrestlers

More Rice?

A sumo wrestler **gets** up at 5:00 A.M. He **trains** for 6 hours. He **has** nothing for breakfast but he **has** lunch at 11:30. He **eats** fifteen bowls of rice. Yes, sumo wrestlers **eat** a lot of rice – so they often **have** heart problems.

Interviewer	So, Mr. Dewanoumi, you **eat** only rice for lunch.
Mitsugu Dewanoumi	No. We **eat** vegetables, fish and meat with the rice. I **have** carrots, potatoes and spinach with my rice.

More Apartments?

In Singapore 90% of people **live** in apartments.

More Speed?

A bullet from a gun **travels** at 8,400 miles per hour.
The earth **travels** at 67,000 miles per hour!

Answer the questions from the texts on page 21 and above.

1 For breakfast sumo wrestlers eat **a** nothing?
                                    b fish?
                                    c rice?
2 In Singapore most people are in apartments. Yes/No?
3 Which is faster? **a** the earth?
                   b a bullet from a gun?

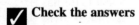 **Check the answers**

4 The verbs in bold are in the *Present Simple*. The *Present Simple* in the texts is for:

a	routines and habits	Yes/No?
b	actions we see now	Yes/No?
c	facts	Yes/No?
d	what is generally true	Yes/No?

Check the answers

5 Match the sentences with the uses of the *Present Simple*.

a In Singapore 90% of people live in apartments. routines and habits
b A sumo wrestler gets up at 5:00 A.M. facts
c The earth travels at 67,000 mph. what is generally true

 Check the answers

Form

6 Look at the verbs in the texts on page 22 and answer the questions.

In the *Present Simple* there is **-s** after

a	'he'	Yes/No?
b	'they'	Yes/No?
c	'you'	Yes/No?
d	'we'	Yes/No?
e	'I'	Yes/No?

7 Complete the table with *eat* or *eats*, *have* or *has*.

Present Simple

I We You They Sumo wrestlers	a *eat*_____ b *h*_____	lunch at 11:30 A.M.
He She It A sumo wrestler	c *e*_____ d *h*_____	

 Check the answers

Tip

A good student says, 'Yes'
To **he**, **she**, **it** with **-s**!

Spelling

8 Complete the spelling rules and spell the verb after *he/she/it*.

a eat   ⇨   eats
After most verbs, add -s   train ⇨ ___*trains*___

b go   ⇨   goes
After -o, add - __ __   do   ⇨ ___*does*___

c fly   ⇨   flies
After consonant + -y, add - __ __ __   cry   ⇨ _____

d pay   ⇨   pays
After vowel + -y, add - __   buy   ⇨ _____

e wash   ⇨   washes
After -sh, add -__ __   rush   ⇨ _____

f watch   ⇨   watches
After -ch, add -__ __   catch ⇨ _____

g kiss   ⇨   kisses
After -ss, add -__ __   miss   ⇨ _____

h fizz   ⇨   fizzes
After -zz, add -__ __   buzz   ⇨ _____

i mix   ⇨   mixes
After -x, add -__ __   relax ⇨ _____

j have   ⇨   has!   have   ⇨ _____
k be   ⇨   is!!   be   ⇨ _____
Some verbs are irregular!

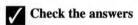 **Check the answers**

⚠Mistakes with -s

9 Put ☑ for a correct sentence and ☒ for an incorrect sentence.

a She has rice for lunch.   ☑   **b** She haves rice for lunch.   ☒
c He have rice for lunch.   ☐   **d** A sumo wrestler has rice for
                                        lunch.   ☐

e	Sumo wrestlers train for 6 hours.	☐	**f** Sumo wrestlers trains for 6 hours.	☐
g	They eats a lot of rice.	☐	**h** They eat a lot of rice.	☐
i	I eat breakfast at 7:00.	☐	**j** I eats breakfast at 7:00.	☐
k	You train for hours.	☐	**l** You trains for hours.	☐
m	We sleeps for 8 hours.	☐	**n** We sleep for 8 hours.	☐
o	Training stops at 11:30.	☐	**p** It stop at 11:30.	☐

✓ Check the answers

⚠Spelling mistakes with -s

10 Correct the spelling mistakes in all the verbs.

a A sumo wrestler studys for hours.   *studies*
b Mr. Dewanoumi saies he eates rice.   _____
c A sumo wrestler finishs training at 11:30.   _____
d My mother gos to sleep at 11:00.   _____
e My father relaxs in the evening and watchs TV. _____
f Romeo kisss Juliet.   _____
g Shake cola and it fizzs!   _____

✓ Check the answers

Practice

11 Make sentences.

a In one lifetime, one person   lose 50–100 hairs.
b In one year, people in Britain   drinks 23 million Coca-Colas.
c In one day, we   drink 73 billion cups of tea.
d In one hour, the world   serve 1 million people.
e In one hour, McDonald's restaurants   watches TV for 12 years.

✓ Check the answers

12 Choose the correct form of the verbs.

In a normal life we **a** sleep/sleeps for 25 years. A teenager **b** sleep/sleeps for 8½ hours. A baby **c** have/has more sleep – it **d** sleep/sleeps for 10 hours. An adult **e** sleep/sleeps for 7 or 8. Older adults **f** have/has only 5 or 6 hours. There **g** is/are two types of sleep. First, you **h** go/goes into deep sleep. Your temperature **i** fall/falls, your body **j** relax/relaxes. After 30 minutes, you **k** is/are in active sleep. Your eyes **l** move/moves and you **m** dream/dreams.

13 Complete the text with the verbs in the correct form. Use the verbs once only.

> ~~walk~~   open   do   do   cook   have   get   drive   go

Some children and adults a *walk* in their sleep and sleepwalkers **b** _____ strange things. They **c** _____ doors and windows. They **d** _____ a bath or a shower. A girl in Wales **e** _____ breakfast in her sleep. She also **f** _____ shopping. A man in Scotland **g** _____ his car and he **h** _____ into bed with other people!

✓ **Check the answers**

Now you

Write about your family in the *Present Simple*. Here are some verbs:

> sleep   get   up   study   work   watch
> eat...for breakfast   have...for lunch   live

a Write one thing everyone does.
  We all _____

b Write one thing only you do.
  I _____

c Write one thing only your mother, father, sister or brother does.
  He/she _____

➤ Unit 5 *Present Simple* (positive and negative)
➤ Unit 7 *Present Simple* (questions)
➤ Unit 8 *Present Simple* + adverbs of frequency
➤ Unit 9 *Present Simple* with *when*
➤ Unit 13 *Present Simple/Present Progressive*

7 Present Simple full verbs (questions)
■ Do you drink?
■ Does she smoke?

Meaning

1 Find the answers to the questions in the text below.

a The family buys all their food from the supermarket. True/False?
b The family buys all their food online. True/False?

The Buying Game

How much do we spend on food? What about London families? **Do they shop** at the big supermarkets or the local [shops/stores]? Sheila Keating interviews a family [in/on] one London street.

Do you buy food every day?
Yes, we do. Usually milk and bread.

Where do you shop?
We buy our milk and bread from the small [shop in/store on] our street.

And the other food? Does it come from the supermarket?
Yes, it does. Most of our food comes from Tesco.

Do you shop online?
Yes, with Tesco Direct every two weeks.

And the delivery from Tesco – does it cost a lot?
No, it doesn't. It costs nothing. The delivery is free, which is nice.

How much do you spend?
About £400 a month online and about £15 a week at our local [shop/store].

Does your daughter help you with the shopping?
Yes, she does. She loves shopping! She buys the milk from our local [shop/store] sometimes.

 Check the answers

Form

2 Complete the tables with the words in the box. The text on page 27 will help you.

| where   does   does   ~~do~~   do   doesn't   don't |

Present Simple: questions

Yes/No questions			
a _Do_	I you we they	shop online	**?**
b ___	he she	help	
	it	cost a lot	

Short answers				
Yes, I you we they	**c** ___	No, I you we they	**e** ___	
he she it	**d** ___	he she it	**f** ___	

Wh- questions		
g ___	do you does she	shop?

✓ **Check the answers**

Tip

Only one *S* with **he/she/it**.
He shop*S* in the supermarket.
Doe*S* he shop in the supermarket?
~~Does he shops~~ in the supermarket?

⚠ Common mistakes

3 Correct the mistakes in the questions.

a She like shopping?
   Does she like shopping?

b Does they spend a lot of money?

_____

c When you shop?

_____

d You buy milk in the supermarket?

_____

e Does she spends a lot?

_____

f When he goes to the supermarket?

_____

✓ **Check the answers**

Practice

4 Match the lines from the songs.

a How do you   me… now that I can dance? (*Brian Poole & the Tremeloes*)

b Why does it always do you, do you want to dance? (*Cliff Richard*)

c Do you love do what you do to me? (*Gerry & the Pacemakers*)

d Do you, do you, rain on me? (*Travis*)

✓ **Check the answers**

5 Match the questions with the answers.

a Where do you live?   He's from Paris.

b Do you smoke?   No, you don't.

c Where does your friend, Pierre, come from?   8:30.

d Do your parents live near you?   Yes, in the next street.

e Do I look tired?   In Hong Kong.

f What time do we leave on Mondays?   Yes, he does.

g Does your brother live at home?   No, I don't.

✓ **Check the answers**

6 Put the words in the correct order to make questions about your daily routine.

a do what get up you time ?   *What time do you get up?*
b a shower or a bath you do have ?   _____
c breakfast eat you do ?   _____
d for lunch you what do have ?   _____
e work finish when you do ?   _____
f you in the evenings do what do ?   _____
g read you in bed do ?   _____

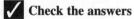 **Check the answers**

7 Look at the information about David and Sally.

	David	Sally
eat meat	✓	✗
smoke	✗	✗
drink	✓	✓
speak Russian	✗	✓
like cooking	✓	✗

Here are the answers to *Yes/No questions* about David and Sally. Write the questions.

a _____ ?
Yes, he does. His [favourite/favorite] is Italian food.

b _____ ?
Yes, she does. She speaks it very well.

c _____ ?
No, she doesn't. She's a vegetarian.

d _____ ?
No, they don't.

e _____ ?
Yes, they do.

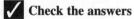 **Check the answers**

8 Write short answers to the questions about David and Sally.

a Does David eat meat? *Yes, he does.*
b Does Sally smoke? _____
c Does David drink? _____
d Does David speak Russian? _____
e Does Sally like cooking? _____

✓ **Check the answers**

9 What about you? Ask someone questions with *Wh-* (*Where, What...?*)

a I live in Cambridge.
  What about you – *where do you live*?
b I get up at 6.30.
  What about you – _____?
c My family live in Edinburgh.
  What about your family – _____?
d My sister works in Washington.
  What about your sister – _____?
e My brother is a psychotherapist.
  What about your brother – _____?

✓ **Check the answers**

Now you

Answer the questions about you. Use short answers.

a Do you eat meat? _____
b Do you drink? _____
c Do you smoke? _____
d Does it rain a lot in your country? _____
e Do your parents live with you? _____
f Does your mother like cooking? _____
g Does your father speak English? _____
h Do you and your family live in a big city? _____

> ➤ Unit 5 *Present Simple* (positive and negative)
> ➤ Unit 6 *Present Simple* third person singular

8 | *Present Simple* with adverbs of frequency
■ I always eat salad

Meaning

1 Answer the questions from the speech bubbles below.

a Who gets the news from a newspaper more than from television? A /B /C /D /E ?

b Who is a vegetarian? A /B /C /D /E ?

c Who wants to be very fit? A /B /C /D /E ?

d Who eats a cold lunch more than a hot lunch? A /B /C /D /E ?

e Who wears informal clothes most of the time? A /B /C /D /E ?

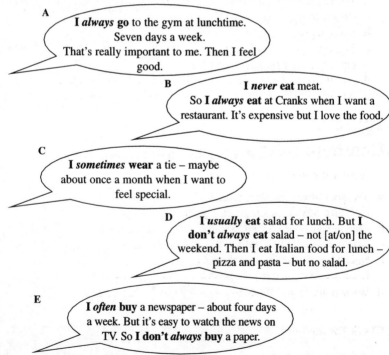

A
I *always* go to the gym at lunchtime. Seven days a week. That's really important to me. Then I feel good.

B
I *never* eat meat. So I *always* eat at Cranks when I want a restaurant. It's expensive but I love the food.

C
I *sometimes* wear a tie – maybe about once a month when I want to feel special.

D
I *usually* eat salad for lunch. But I don't *always* eat salad – not [at/on] the weekend. Then I eat Italian food for lunch – pizza and pasta – but no salad.

E
I *often* buy a newspaper – about four days a week. But it's easy to watch the news on TV. So I don't *always* buy a paper.

✓ **Check the answers**

**2 Put the *frequency adverbs* from the texts in the correct boxes.
Look at the texts to help you.**

~~always~~ never often sometimes usually

100%	70%	60%	30%	0%
a	**b**	**c**	**d**	**e**
always				

✓ Check the answers

Form

3 Look back at the texts on page 32 and answer these questions.

a Which tense is in **bold** – the *Present Simple* or the *Present Progressive*?

b Is the tense for repeated actions?

c The *adverbs* in ***bold italic*** are *frequency adverbs*. Are the *adverbs* before or after the main verb?

d Are the *adverbs* before or after the subject pronoun (I)?

e Are the *adverbs* before or after the negative verb (don't)?

✓ Check the answers

⚠Common mistakes

4 Correct the mistakes.

a She goes always to the gym.
   She always goes to the gym.

b They always don't eat salad.

_____

c Never I go to the [theatre/theater].

_____

d We usually to go by bus.

_____

✓ Check the answers

Practice

5 Put the words in the correct order to make sentences about our usual [holiday/vacation].

a always Italy to go we in August
We always go to Italy in August.

b sometimes there we drive

_____

c often on stay a campsite we

_____

d never children us come with the

_____

e spend usually week we one there

_____

 Check the answers

6 Look at the information about the Hall family – Sheila and Fred and their children.

	Sheila and Fred	Andrew	Susan
eat breakfast	100%	0%	30%
go shopping	70%	0%	60%
do the dishes	70%	0%	60%

Write about the family. Use *always, usually, often, sometimes, never*.

a Sheila and Fred *always eat breakfast.*
b Andrew _____
c Susan _____
d Sheila and Fred _____
e Andrew _____
f Susan _____
g Sheila and Fred _____
h Andrew _____
i Susan _____

 Check the answers

Now you

Answer the questions about you. Use a frequency adverb.

a What's the first thing you do in the morning?
b What's the last thing you do at night?
c What do you have for breakfast?
d Do you go to the gym?
e Do you wear a tie?
f Do you eat meat?
g Do you eat salad?
h Do you buy a newspaper?
i What does your family do on [holiday/vacation]?

➢ Unit 5 *Present Simple* (positive and negative)
➢ Unit 6 *Present Simple* third person singular
➢ Unit 7 *Present Simple* (questions)

9 | *Present Simple with when*
■ When I get old, will you love me?

Meaning

1 Here is a poem about love. Do you think a mother is talking to her son? Or a husband is talking to his wife?

♥♥♥♥♥♥♥♥♥♥♥♥♥♥♥♥♥♥♥♥♥♥♥♥♥♥♥♥♥♥♥♥♥♥♥

Love is when...

When I'm older, will you love me?
When I'm older, won't you care?
Will you kiss me, won't you hold me?
Will you still be there?

Are you going to make me cups of tea **when I get** very old?
Are you going to drive me to the sea **when the weather's** cold?

When I get old, will you still love me?
When I get old, won't you still care?
Will you like me, won't you need me?
Will you still be there?

♥♥♥♥♥♥♥♥♥♥♥♥♥♥♥♥♥♥♥♥♥♥♥♥♥♥♥♥♥♥♥♥♥♥♥

✅ Check the answer

2 Answer the questions about *when* in the poem.

a Which tense comes after *when*? *Present Simple* or a Future Form?
b There is a comma (**,**) if the *when*-clause is first. True/False?
c There is a comma (**,**) if the *when*-clause is second. True/False?
d Is the phrase *When I'm older* about the past, present or future?
e Is the phrase *When I get old* about the past, present or future?

f Is the phrase *When the weather's cold* about the past, present, or future?

g *When* is for things which are sure to happen. True/False?

✔ **Check the answers**

Form

3 Complete the table with the words in the box.

| ~~won't~~ | get | care | will | make |

When	I 'm older, I **b** _____ old	**a** _____ you love me ? **c** *won't* you **d** _____ me tea? are you going to **e** _____ ?

✔ **Check the answers**

⚠ Common mistakes

4 Correct the mistakes.

a When I will be in London next week, I'm going to visit the British Museum.

_____

b When I arrive at the station later, I phone you.

_____

✔ **Check the answers**

Practice

5 Match the lines from these songs.

a Will you still feed me   I'm going to hold you tight. *Beatles*

b When I fall in love,   when I'm 64? *Beatles*

c When I get home tonight,   it will be forever. *Johnny Mathis*

✔ **Check the answers**

.

6 Complete the blanks. Use the verbs in brackets. The sentences are all about the future. Use *will/won't* or the *Present Simple*.

a I'*ll phone* you when I _____ (*get*) home from school.
b We're going to Germany tomorrow. I _____ (*tell*) you all about it when we _____ (*come*) back.
c I don't want to leave without you. I _____ (*wait*) and go when you _____ (*be*) ready.
d I'm going to bed when I _____ (*finish*) my homework.
e When I _____ (*arrive*), I _____ (*send*) you a postcard.

✅ **Check the answers**

Now you

Write true sentences about you, tomorrow or this week.

a *When I* _____
b *When* _____

➤ Unit 11 *Present Progressive* for future arrangements
➤ Unit 19 *going to* future

10 | *Imperative (positive and negative)*
■ Turn left
■ Don't turn right

Meaning

1 Read the directions in the conversation. Answer the question: Are the directions correct?

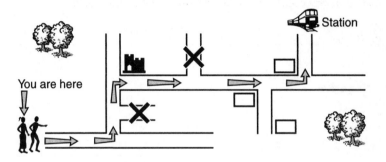

A	Excuse me, can you tell me the way to the station, please?
B	**Go** [straight on/straight]. **Turn** left. Then **turn** right... no, **don't turn** right.
A	OK.
B	**Take** the second street on the right.
A	OK.
B	Then **take** the first street on the left. No, wait a minute, **don't take** the first street on the left, **take** the second. And the station is in front of you, at the end of the street.
A	Thank you very much.
B	You're welcome.

 Check the answer

2 The verbs in bold are in the *Imperative.* Here the *Imperative* is used to give directions. True or False?

 Check the answer

Form

3 Complete the table. The dialogue on page 39 will help you. Use the words in the box below.

~~turn~~	don't	take	take

The Imperative

Positive	Go		[straight on/straight]
	a *Turn*		left right
	b _____		the first street on the right the second street on the left
Negative		go	[straight on/straight]
	c _____	turn	left right
		d ___	the first street on the right the second street on the left

 Check the answers

More meanings

4 Match the uses of the *Imperative* to the examples.

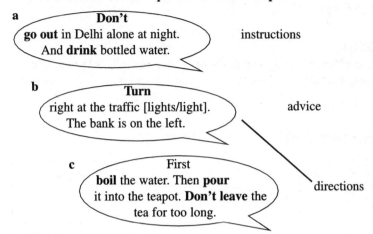

a

Don't go out in Delhi alone at night. And **drink** bottled water.

instructions

b

Turn right at the traffic [lights/light]. The bank is on the left.

advice

c

First **boil** the water. Then **pour** it into the teapot. **Don't leave** the tea for too long.

directions

Tip

It is not polite to use the *Imperative* for requests. Use 'Could you..., please?'

✗ Give me the sugar.

✔ Could you pass me the sugar, please?

Common mistakes

5 Correct the mistakes.

a Don't to go out alone at night   *Don't go out alone at night*

b Go you by bus.   _____

c Not wait here.   _____

d Go not [straight on/straight].   _____

✔ **Check the answers**

Practice

6 Match the lines from the famous songs.

a ˙Mama don't   with me because you're playing with fire.
                           (*Rolling Stones*)

b Don't play   don't go… (*Van Morrison*)

c Baby please   me this way. (*Communards*)

d Don't leave   go; Daddy, please come home. (*John Lennon*)

 Check the answers

7 Be Creative! Match the parts of the sentences.

a Paint   a novel.
b Write   a bridge.
c Construct   a film.
d Direct   a ten-lane [motorway/highway].
e Build   a picture.

8 Health advice. Write four sentences. Give advice for good health. Use the words in the circle.

a *Don't drink alcohol.*
b _____
c _____
d _____

 Check the answers

Now you

Give directions from your home to the nearest [shop/store] or station or bus stop.

_____

_____

_____

_____

Write two sentences to give advice to a visitor to your country. Use the *Imperative* – write one positive and one negative sentence.

a _____

b *Don't* _____

11

Present Progressive for future arrangements (positive, negative and questions)

■ We're meeting here at eight

Meaning

1 Answer the questions about the dialogue.
Two friends, A and B, have a conversation.

a Is A free tonight?   Yes/No?
b Is B free tonight?   Yes/No?

A How about a film tonight?
B Tonight?
A Yes.
B Oh, sorry – **I'm going** to a jazz club.
A The *606*?
B No, **I'm not going** there. Look, here are the tickets. **Charlie's coming** with me.
A Charlie?
B Yes, **we're meeting** here at 8:00.
A Where **are you going**?
B *Ronnie Scotts*. What about Tina and Jane?
A **They're staying at home.** OK. Another time. I'll watch TV.
B OK. Sorry.

✓ **Check your answers**

2 Answer the questions about the grammar in the dialogue.

a What tense is **in bold** in the dialogue? *Present Simple/Future Simple/Present Progressive*?
b Is the tense for the present or the future?

c Is the tense for an arrangement or a new idea?

d Is the tense for a decision now or a decision from the past?

✓ **Check your answers**

Form

3 Look at the dialogue and complete the table.

Present Progressive: for future

I	**a** *'m*	(not)	
He She **b** ____ Charlie		(not) (n't)	going to a jazz club tonight.
We You **c** ____ They			
What	**d** ____	you doing tonight?	

⚠ Common mistakes

4 Correct the <u>underlined</u> mistakes. The tense is wrong.

a **A** Are you free tonight? **B** No, <u>I go out</u>.   *I'm going out.*

b <u>Do you watch</u> the [match/game] tomorrow? _____

c <u>She doesn't come</u> to the party next week.   _____

d **A** Would you like to go to the [cinema/movies]?
   B Sorry, <u>I go</u> to John's house.   _____

✓ **Check the answers**

Tip

Learn two useful questions:
'Are you doing anything tonight?'
'What are you doing on Monday?'

Practice

5 Look at Ann's [diary/calendar] and put the dialogue in the correct order.

```
┌─────────────────────────────┐
│ Monday                      │
│ ─────────────────────────   │
│ ─────────────────────────   │
│ ─────────────────────────   │
│                             │
│ Tuesday                     │
│ ─────────────────────────   │
│ ───────Jean──────────────   │
│ ─────────────────────────   │
│                             │
│ Wednesday                   │
│ ─────────────────────────   │
│ ─────────────────────────   │
│ ─────────────────────────   │
└───∨∨∨∨∨∨∨───────────────────┘
```

a Pete: What about Wednesday?
b Pete: Good. I'm cooking for some friends. Would you like to come?
c Pete: Are you busy on Tuesday?
d Ann: No, I'm free all day. I'm not doing anything.
e Ann: Yes, I'm afraid so. I'm meeting Jean.
f Ann: That would be great. Thanks.

6 Put the words in the correct order.

a leaving/at 3:00/you/are/?   *Are you leaving at 3:00?*
b aren't/on Friday/to Paris/flying/we   _____
c they/when/arriving/are/?   _____
d all next week/'m/working/I   _____
e taxi/soon/your/'s/arriving   _____
f to LA/travelling/is/how/she/?   _____

7 Here are Jon's tickets. Complete his conversation with a friend.

```
ADULT                    £5.30
[Cinema/Movie]
   Showing at 8:40 P.M.
   Monday [10 July/July 10]
Screen: 2
```

```
ADMIT ONE
Ronnie Scott's
Saturday [15 July/July 15]
```

Steve   What   **a** _____ on Saturday?
Jon   I'm   **b** _____ Ronnie Scott's.
Steve   Are you free on Monday night?
Jon   No,   **c** _____

Now you

Write about three of your plans for this week or next week. Say *what*,
where and *when*.

a *I'm* _____
b *I* _____
c _____

➤ Unit 12 *Present Progressive* for now

12 Present Progressive for now (positive and negative)

■ He's working
■ I'm not working

Meaning

1 Anne calls to speak to someone at the BBC. She speaks to the receptionist. Who does she speak to after that? Is it

        a   Paul?

        b   Sheila?

        c   John?

        d   Peter?

        e   nobody?

Anne	Could I speak to Paul Jenkins, please?
Receptionist	One minute, please. I'm sorry, Paul's busy at the moment. **He isn't answering his phone.** I think **he's recording** in the studio.
Anne	OK. What about Sheila Jones? Is she there?
Receptionist	Sheila? No, I'm afraid Sheila's busy now, too. **She's talking** to the director.
Anne	All right. And John Smith and Peter Davies? Are they free at the moment?
Receptionist	Err… Oh, John and Peter – **they aren't working** now – they're at the restaurant. **They're having** a coffee break.
Anne	What's that noise?
Receptionist	Oh, no! That's the fire alarm! We're all busy now. Can you call back?

✓ **Check the answer**

2 The verbs in bold are in the *Present Progressive*.

a In the dialogue, the *Present Progressive* is for actions in progress now, at the moment. True/False?

b In the dialogue, the *Present Progressive* is for habits and routines. True/False?

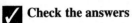 Check the answers

Form

3 Complete the table with the words in the box. Use the dialogue on page 48 to help you.

n't	n't	are	is	~~'m~~

Present Progressive – positive and negative

I	**a** *'m*	(not)	
He She It	**b** ____	**d** (____)	working now.
We You They	**c** ____	**e** (____)	

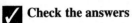 Check the answers

Spelling

4 Complete the spelling rules and spell the verbs with *-ing*.

a wear → wearing

Most verbs add ___ ***ing***   work → ***working***

b smoke → smoking

Verbs + -e: lose _____   write → _____

c lie → lying

Verbs + -ie: -ie changes to ____   die → _____

d run → running
Verbs with one syllable and one vowel + one consonant: double the consonant

stop → _____

e prefer → preferring
Long verbs with a final stressed syllable and one vowel + one consonant: double the consonant

begin → _____

⚠Common mistakes

5 Correct the mistakes.

a Look – she's comeing.
Look – she's coming.

b I writing a letter now.

_____

c You're runing too fast.

_____

d The cat's sleeping.

_____

e They not listening to me.

_____

f I amn't doing my homework at the moment.

_____

✓ Check the answers

Practice

6 Match the lines from the famous songs.

a I am   blowing in the wind. (*Bob Dylan*)
b The answer is   is give peace a chance. (*John Lennon*)
c I'm dreaming   sailing. (*Rod Stewart*)
d All we are saying   strawberry fields. (*The Beatles*)
e She   of a white Christmas. (*Bing Crosby*)
f …we're going to   's leaving home, bye, bye. (*The Beatles*)

✓ Check the answers

7 Make four sentences in the *Present Progressive* using the words in the circle. You can use the words more than once.

a *She's laughing* _____
b _____
c _____
d _____

☑ **Check the answers**

8 Fill in the blanks with the verbs in the box. Use the *Present Progressive*.

read	~~sit~~	do	play	work	enjoy	do

It's 6 o'clock and Eddie Riddell, 45, **a** *is sitting* in his house near Los Angeles. He **b** _____ a story to his son, Matt, aged 6. His daughter, Emma, aged 4, **c** _____ with her toys. Eddie has two older children – Jonathan and Luke. They **d** _____ their homework upstairs. Eddie is a 'househusband'. His wife, Rose, **e** _____ late at a bank in Encino. 'At the moment I **f** _____ life at home,' says Eddie. 'And Rose is happy with her job at the bank. We **g** _____ what we want to do.'

☑ **Check the answers**

Now you

Write true sentences about you now.
For example: I/wear/suit
            I'm not wearing a suit. or I'm wearing a suit.

a I/eat _____
b I/learn English _____
c It/rain _____

d The sun/shine _____

e I/do/housework _____

f I/wear/jeans _____

g My father/work _____

h My parents/watch TV _____

✓ **Check the answers**

➤ Unit 11 *Present Progressive* for future arrangements
➤ Unit 13 *Present Simple* and *Present Progressive*

13 | *Present Simple* and *Present Progressive*
■ I live in Egypt
■ I'm visiting Australia

Meaning

1 Find the answers to the questions in the text.

a Find three permanent things about Peter Simons' life.

b Find two temporary things about Peter Simons' life.

> Peter Simons **works** as a film director. Peter **lives** in Los Angeles. He **makes** one film every year. At the moment **he's directing** a new film in India. **He's working** in Delhi on a film about Gandhi.

✓ **Check the answers**

2 There are two tenses in bold in the text – the *Present Simple* and the *Present Progressive*.

a **He works** is *Present Simple*. Find two more verbs in the *Present Simple*. _____ _____

b **He's directing** is *Present Progressive*. Find one more verb in the *Present Progressive*. _____

c Which tense is for something permanent and which tense is for something temporary?

3 Match the questions with the answers.

a What do you do? (*permanent job*) ⟍   In a hotel for the moment.

b What are you doing? (*temporary action*) ⟍ In Bombay.

c Where do you live? (*permanent address*)   I work for a computer company.

d Where are you living? (*temporary address*) Looking for my dictionary.

4 Put the meanings in the box with the correct tense.

temporary things	habits	~~actions now~~	routines
	permanent things		

The *Present Simple* is for	The *Present Progressive* is for
	actions now

 Check the answers

Form

For the form of the *Present Simple* and the *Present Progressive* see Units 5, 6, 7 and 12.

⚠Common mistakes

5 Correct the mistakes.

a Where you usually work?
  Where do you usually work? _____

b She go swimming every day.
  _____

c He is speaks Polish.
  _____

d They like not football
  _____

e Wait – I come.
  _____

f Look – he walking very fast.
  _____

g I'm drive to the airport at the moment.
  _____

h We no eat fish.
  _____

i What you doing there?

_____

j Jean is busy – she's [have/take] a bath.

_____

✓ **Check the answers**

Practice

6 Choose the correct tense.

a **A** Do you eat meat?/~~Are you eating meat?~~ Do you eat meat? _is correct_

   B No, I'm a vegetarian.

b **A** How do you do?/How are you doing?

   B Nice to meet you.

c **A** Do you eat meat?/Are you eating meat?

   B Do you want some?

d **A** What do you do?/What are you doing?

   B I'm a taxi driver.

e **A** What do you do?/What are you doing?

   B I'm reading the newspaper.

f **A** It rains/It's raining.

   B We can't go out now.

g **A** Where's Andy?

   B He's watching TV./He watches TV.

h **A** What language are you speaking?/What language do you speak?

   B Japanese – I'm on the telephone with Kyoko in Tokyo.

i **A** Can I turn off the radio?

   B Yes, I don't listen to it./Yes, I'm not listening to it.

j **A** The sun is shining/The sun shines.

   B Yes, it's a lovely day.

✓ **Check the answers**

7 Put the verbs in brackets in the _Present Simple_ or the _Present Progressive_.

a Excuse me, **_do you speak_** (you/speak) Spanish? A little.

b 'Where's Emma?' 'She _____ ([have/take]) a bath at the moment.'

c Listen! Someone _____ (play) the guitar next door.

d What time _____ (you/get up) every day?
e The telephone _____ (ring)!
f Sue is busy. She _____ (do) her homework.
g They _____ (not watch) TV very often.

✓ **Check the answers**

Now you

Write about two permanent things in your life. Use the *Present Simple*.

a _____
b _____

Write about two temporary things in your life. Use the *Present Progressive*.

a _____
b _____

➤ Unit 5 *Present Simple* (positive and negative)
➤ Unit 6 *Present Simple* third person singular
➤ Unit 7 *Present Simple* (questions)
➤ Unit 11 *Present Progressive* for future arrangements
➤ Unit 12 *Present Progressive* for now

14 *Past Simple be* (positive, negative and questions)
- I was at work
- They were at school
- Were you by the bank?

Meaning

1 Read the conversation about a car accident last Tuesday.

a Is A or B the policeman?
b Is A or B the witness?

A Mrs. B., where **were you** at the time of the accident? **Were you** by the bank?

B The bank? No, **I wasn't** by the bank. **I was** outside the [cinema/movies].

A What time **was the accident** last Tuesday?

B **It was** at 3 o'clock.

A And how many **people were** in the accident?

B **A young woman was** on the bicycle. And **three people were** in the car – the driver and two men.

A And where **were the two men** exactly?

B **They were** in the back of the car.

A And **were you** alone outside the [cinema/movies]?

B No, **I was** with my husband. **We were** in [the queue/line] for tickets.

 Check the answers

The accident was in the past – last Tuesday. The verbs **in bold** are about finished actions in the past. They are the *Past Simple* of the verb *be*.

Form

2 Complete the table. The dialogue will help. Use the words in the box.

| was   was   wasn't   were   were |

Past Simple: *be*

Positive		Negative		Question		
I He She **a** *was* It		I He She **c** _____ It		**d** _____	I he she it	
	OK.		OK.			OK?
We You **b** _____ They		We You weren't They		**e** _____	we you they	

n't is short for **not**. Use **n't** in informal and spoken English.

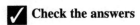 Check the answers

⚠ Common mistakes

3 Correct the mistakes.

a Was you outside the [cinema/movies]?
   Were you outside the [cinema/movies]?

b She not was in the car.
   _____

c They was outside the bank.
   _____

d I weren't in the car.
   _____

e My wife and I was in the back of the car.
   _____

f Was the people in the car men or women?
   _____

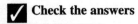 Check the answers

Practice

4 Write ten sentences. Use the words in the circle. Use the words more than once.

a   *Were you late?*
b   _____
c   _____
d   _____
e   _____
f   _____
g   _____
h   _____
i   _____
j   _____

✓ **Check the answers**

5 Fill in the blanks with *was* or *were*.

a   Viscountess Astor   *was*   the first female member of the British parliament. She _____ North American by birth.

b   In 1911 the average speed of traffic in London _____ 17 [kilometres/kilometers] per hour. In 1999 the average speed _____ 17 kph.

c   In 1666 the pronunciation of 'tea' in England _____ 'tay'.

d   Aberdeen, Glasgow and Dublin _____ popular first names in the U.S.A. in 1880.

e   The walls of Babylon _____ 26 [metres/meters] thick.

f   Queen Victoria _____ the queen of England for 54 years.

g   Laszlo Biro, a Hungarian, _____ the inventor of the ballpoint pen.

✓ **Check the answers**

6 Complete the blanks with: *was/wasn't/were/weren't*

Everything **was** wrong!

Last summer we **a** _____ on [holiday in/vacation at] a terrible hotel. The room **b** _____ very small and it **c** _____ very clean. The hotel telephone **d** _____ connected – so no phone calls! The waiters and receptionists **e** _____ very helpful. The food **f** _____ very hot. And finally the weather **g** _____ very nice – it **h** _____ cold and wet. I **i** _____ happy.

 Check the answers

Now you

Write true sentences about you, your partner, your friend, or your family in the past. Write about yesterday. Use the *Past Simple* of *be*. Write two positive and two negative sentences.

a *Yesterday I was* _____

b _____

c _____

d _____

➤ Unit 15 *Past Simple – there was/there were*
➤ Unit 16 *Past Simple* regular verbs
➤ Unit 17 *Past Simple* regular and irregular verbs
➤ Unit 18 *Past Simple* (questions and negative)

15 Past Simple – there was/ there were (positive, negative and questions)

- There was a large population
- There were millions
- Were there any mobile phones?

Meaning

1 Match the titles to the texts.

a Technology

b People

c Politics

Big changes 1970–2000

I

In 1970 **there were** 3.5 billion people in the world. In 2000 **there was** a population of 6 billion. A big change.

II

In 1970 **there weren't** any mobile phones in the world. But **were there** any mobile phones around in 2000? Yes, **there were** – millions, in fact. A big change.

III

In 1970 **there was** still a wall between East and West Berlin. In 2000 **there wasn't** a wall between East and West Berlin. A big change.

 Check the answers

The texts talk about finished situations in the past. The verbs in **bold** are in the *Past Simple*.

Form

2 Complete the tables. Use the words in the box. The texts will help.

were   were   ~~was~~   was   n't

Past Simple: positive and negative

There	**a** *was*	**c** (_____)	a population of 3.6 million. a Berlin Wall.
	b _____		1 million people. millions of mobile phones.

Past Simple: question

Questions			**Short Answers**
d _____	there	a mobile phone?	Yes, there was. No, there wasn't.
e _____		any mobile phones?	Yes, there were. No, there weren't.

n't is short for **not**. Use **n't** in informal and spoken English.

✓ Check the answers

⚠ Common mistakes

3 Correct the mistakes.

a There was thousands of people in Rio de Janeiro.
   There were thousands of people in Rio de Janeiro.

b Were mobile phones in New Zealand in 1990?

   _____

c There not were any videos before 1965.

   _____

✓ Check the answers

Practice

4 Complete the blanks with *there was / there wasn't / was there / were there / there were / there weren't*.

a I swim every day but ***there wasn't*** a swimming pool [in/at] the hotel.

b _____ any letters at the reception desk for me today? No, _____

c _____ a rock band in the hotel last night. They were excellent.

d The mini-bar was empty! _____ any drinks in it.

e _____ many people at breakfast? No, not many.

f _____ an art gallery near the hotel but _____ enough time to visit it.

g We were always late for dinner. _____ a lot of traffic.

h The bathroom was wonderful but _____ any towels!

✓ **Check the answers**

5 History Quiz. Complete the blanks to make true sentences. Use *was, were, wasn't, weren't*.

a There ***weren't*** any radios in the 1800s.

b There _____ a wall between East and West Berlin in 1990.

c There _____ dinosaurs 100 million years ago.

d There _____ nine countries in the European Community in 1973.

e There _____ a revolution in France in 1889.

f There _____ two world wars in the twentieth century.

g There _____ any women in *The Beatles* pop group.

h There _____ two men on the moon in 1969.

✓ **Check the answers**

Now you

Write four sentences about your house or your [flat/apartment]. You can use the words in the box.

mobile phones   a [video player/VCR]   a [colour/color] TV
a sauna   a radio   servants   pets   parties   a lot of people

a When I was a child, there was _____ in my [flat/apartment]/house.

b When I was a child, there wasn't _____ in my _____

c When I was a child, there were _____ in my_____
d When I was a child, there weren't any _____in my_____

➢ Unit 3 *there is/ there are* (positive and negative)
➢ Unit 4 *is there?/are there?* (questions)
➢ Unit 14 *Past Simple – be*
➢ Unit 16 *Past Simple* regular verbs
➢ Unit 17 *Past Simple* regular and irregular verbs
➢ Unit 18 *Past Simple* (questions and negative)

16 | *Past Simple* regular verbs (positive)
■ I worked

Meaning

1 Here is a true story. Read the story and answer the question.

Mr Homer Lawyer goes into a bank in the U.S.A. He gives the assistant a bag with a note. The note asks for money. Is this a good idea? Yes or No?

> In 1985 an American, Homer Lawyer, **planned** to rob a bank in Miami. He **travelled** to Miami and **arrived** at the bank. Mr. Lawyer **preferred** cash. He **handed** a bag with a note to the assistant. In the note Mr. Lawyer **asked** for cash. Mr. Lawyer **hurried** home with the bag full of money. Later the bank manager **noticed** Mr. Lawyer's name and address on the back of the note!

✓ **Check the answer**

The story of Homer Lawyer is about completed past actions. So the verbs in **bold** are in the *Past Simple*.

Form

2 Look at the verbs in bold in the story. They are regular verbs in the *Past Simple*. Here are the infinitives – write the *Past Simple* forms from the story.

Infinitive		*Past Simple* – regular verbs
hand	**a**	*handed*
ask	**b**	_____
arrive	**c**	_____
notice	**d**	_____

hurry	e	_____
travel	f	_____
prefer	g	_____
plan	h	_____

 Check the answers

3 The regular verbs in the *Past Simple* end in *-ed*. Yes or No?

 Check the answer

Spelling

4 Complete the spelling rules and spell the verbs.

a ask → ask**ed**

For most verbs: add *-ed*   play   → *played*

b arrive → arriv**ed**

For verbs with **-e**: add - __   save   → _____

c hurry → hurr**ied**

For verbs with consonant + -y:

change **-y** to - __ and add **-ed**   study → _____

d travel → travel**led**

For verbs with **-l** add - __ and add **-ed**   cancel → _____

e prefer → prefer**red**

For long verbs with a final stressed syllable

and one vowel + one consonant:

double the final _____   regret → _____

f plan → plan**ned**

For verbs with consonant + vowel + consonant:

double the final _____   stop   → _____

 Check the answers

Tip

| For the *Simple Past*,
| Add -**ed** last.

Practice

5 Complete the sentences with the correct verb from the brackets. Put the verb in the *Past Simple*.

Unusual facts from the past

a In 1981 Country Bill White ***lived*** for 20 weeks in a coffin. (*live/walk*)

b In 1982 David Scott _____ the piano for 50 days and 18 hours. (*play/swallow*)

c Count Desmond from America _____ 13 swords. (*swallow/terrify*)

d In 1974 a French man, Philippe Petit, _____ people in the street in New York. (*terrify/play*)

e He _____ across a 40-yard wire between the towers of the World Trade Center. (*live/walk*)

f In 1980 Callinatercy Soccer Club _____ [football/soccer] for 65 hours and 1 minute. (*play/walk*)

✓ **Check the answers**

6 Complete the sentences with the correct verb. Put the verb in the *Past Simple*.

More unusual facts from the past

travel	rob	start	pull	prefer

a In Queensland, Australia, thirty-five policemen _____ over 500 [metres/meters] on one motorcycle.

b In Toronto, Canada, Terry McGaurant _____ to ride his motorbike up the 1760 steps of the Canadian National Tower.

c In 1984 two teenagers in England _____ a shop in Yeovil. They _____ the cash register from the wall. The cash register _____ to make a noise – the noise of a burglar alarm!

✓ **Check the answers**

Time expressions

Time expressions with the *Past Simple*.

at	7 o'clock the weekend (British)

on	Saturday [3rd June/June 3rd] the weekend (American)

in	May 1987

last	Wednesday week

3 weeks 4 months	ago

Now you

Write about your past in the *Past Simple*. Here are some verbs:

live	travel	play	walk	arrive

a *I* _____

b _____

c _____

➤ Unit 17 *Past Simple* regular and irregular verbs
➤ Unit 18 *Past Simple* (questions and negative)

17 | *Past Simple* regular and irregular verbs (positive)

- He wrote
- She offered

Meaning

1 Answer the question about the true story below. A New York bank offered a three-year-old child a credit card. Why?

> ### Credit card for a child
>
> In 1999 Charter One bank in New York **wrote** to a three-year old girl, Alessandra Scalise. The bank **offered** her a platinum credit card. They **gave** her a $7000 limit on the card. Why? Alessandra's mother, Antonia, **filled** in the form for the credit card as a joke. There **was** no signature on the form because Alessandra doesn't know how to write her name.
>
> Mrs. Scalise **replied** to the bank for her daughter, 'Thanks for the great offer but I'm only three. I'd like to buy more toys but [Mum/Mom] says when I'm older.' A spokesman, George McCane, **said** the bank **made** a mistake. It **was** 'human error'.

✓ **Check the answer**

The story is about completed actions in the past, so the verbs in **bold** are in the *Past Simple*.

Form

2 All the verbs in bold are regular *Past Simple* and add *-ed*. Yes or No?

✓ **Check the answer**

3 Complete the lists of verbs from the story on page 69.

Regular verbs (+ -ed)	
Infinitive	**Past Simple**
offer	*offered*
fill	_____
reply	_____

Irregular verbs (no -ed)	
Infinitive	**Past Simple**
write	_____
give	_____
be/is	_____
say	_____
make	_____

✓ **Check the answers**

4 Look at the table below. Is the *Past Simple* form the same for all persons? Yes/No?

I	
He	(*regular*)
She	replied to the bank.
It	
We	(*irregular*)
You	made a mistake.
They	

✓ **Check the answer**

5 More irregular verbs.
Match the *Past Simple* forms in the box to the *infinitives*.

a	do	→	*did*	
b	drink	→	_____	
c	fly	→	_____	
d	go	→	_____	
e	have	→	_____	
f	leave	→	_____	
g	run	→	_____	
h	see	→	_____	
i	spend	→	_____	
j	swim	→	_____	
k	take	→	_____	

had
went
took
~~did~~
flew
ran
swam
drank
saw
left
spent

✓ **Check the answer**

Tip

| You can put some irregular verbs (not all) in groups.

6 Put the verbs in the correct group and fill in the *Past Simple* forms.

| ~~drink~~ | spend | leave | write |

a		**b**		**c**	
/iː/ →	/ɪ /	-end →	-ent	/aɪ/ →	/əʊ/
meet	met	send	sent	drive	drove
mean	meant	lend	lent	ride	rode
_____	_____	_____	_____	_____	_____

d

/ɪ/ →	/æ/
sink	sank
swim	swam
drink	_____

✔ Check the answers

⚠ Common mistakes

7 Put ☑ for a correct sentence and ☒ for an incorrect sentence.

a I runned to the bank.	☒	**b** I ran to the bank.	☐
c She walked home.	☐	**d** She walk home.	☐
e They goed to New York.	☐	**f** They went to New York.	☐

✔ Check the answers

Practice

8 Complete the sentences with the verbs in the correct form of the *Past Simple*.

| drink | swim |

Twelve-year-old Thomas Gregg from London was the youngest to swim the English Channel. He **a** _____ the 50 [kilometres/kilometers] in 11 hours 35 minutes. He **b** _____ hot tomato soup because it was so cold.

spend	take	see

Bill and Simone Butler **c** _____ 66 days at sea on a liferaft. A fishing boat **d** _____ them and **e** _____ them home.

leave	have	fly

Charles Linbergh **f** _____ from New York to Paris on the first non-stop solo flight across the Atlantic. He **g** _____ New York with many bottles of water but only five sandwiches. He still **h** _____ three sandwiches in Paris 33 hours later.

✓ **Check the answers**

Now you

Write about your past.

a Write one thing you did yesterday.

I _____

b Write one thing you did last week.

I _____

c Write one thing you did on your last [holiday/vacation].

I _____

➤ Unit 16 *Past Simple* regular verbs
➤ Unit 18 *Past Simple* (questions and negative)

18 Past Simple (questions and negative)
- Did he work?
- He didn't sing

Meaning

1 Find the answer to the question in the true story about three bank robbers in Scotland.

The robbers left the bank with
- **a** £5,000?
- **b** £500?
- **c** 50p?
- **d** nothing?

In 1975 three men **went** into a bank in Scotland. **Did they go** in to pay their bills? No, **they didn't go** in for that. **Did they want** to open a bank account? No, **they didn't want** to join the bank. Well, **what did they want**? In fact, **they wanted** to rob the bank. First, they asked the cashiers for £5000. But the cashiers **didn't believe** them. Then the men asked for £500. **Did they give** them the money? No, **the cashiers didn't give** it to them. **They gave** them nothing – they only laughed. Next, the men asked for £50 and then 50 pence. The cashiers laughed again. Finally, the men got trapped in the revolving doors on their way out.

 Check the answer

Form

2 Complete the tables on the next page using the words in the box. Use the story to help you.

did	gave	give	want	didn't

	Positive
I	
He	wanted money.
She	**a** _____ £500.
The robber	
We	**Negative**
You	
They	didn't **b** _____ money.
The cashiers	**c** _____ give £500.

Questions		
Did	I he she the robber we you they the robbers	**d** _____ money? give £500?
What	**e** _____ she they	want?

✓ Check the answers

3 Answer the questions about the form of the *Past Simple* in questions and the negative.

a We use ***did*** to make questions in the *Past Simple*. True/False?

b We use ***did*** to make the negative in the *Past Simple*. True/False?

c Which is correct – 'She didn't arrive.' or 'She didn't arrived.'?

d Which is correct – 'He didn't left.' or 'He didn't leave.'?

e Which is correct – 'Did they went?' or 'Did they go?'

✓ Check the answers

⚠ Common mistakes

4 Correct the mistakes in the negative and the questions.

a I not came.   *I didn't come.*
b He no arrived.   _____
c She didn't liked tea.   _____
d Did we bought it here?   _____
e Did they lived in Scotland?   _____
f They not saw me.   _____

✓ **Check the answers**

Practice

5 False facts I. Complete the sentences with the positive form of the verb.

a I didn't go to Los Angeles, I *went* to Santa Barbara.
b We didn't meet Ann, we _____ Max.
c She didn't leave yesterday, she _____ last Thursday.
d We didn't see John, we _____ Jean.
e The film didn't begin at 8:30, it _____ at 9:30.
f You didn't arrive at 5:00 you _____ at 6:00.

✓ **Check the answers**

6 False facts II. All the sentences have wrong information. Make them positive or negative to correct the information.

a Prince Charles became king of England in 1999.
   Prince Charles didn't become king of England in 1999.
b The Niagara Falls in Canada didn't freeze completely in 1925.

   _____

c Napoleon Bonaparte didn't design the Italian flag.

   _____

d The U.S.A. had a national anthem before 1931.

   _____

e The *Titanic* sank in 1955.

   _____

f The Second World War ended in 1944.

   _____

7 [Holiday/vacation] questions I. Put the words in the correct order to make questions.

a where for your last [holiday/vacation] go you did?
Where did you go for your last [holiday/vacation]?

b plane go you did by?

_____

c cost the [holiday/vacation] much how did?

_____

d when you get back did?

_____

e good have time you did a?

_____

✓ **Check the answers**

8 [Holiday/vacation] questions II. Complete the questions in this dialogue.

A I got back from a [holiday/vacation] last week.
B a Where *did you go*?
A Paris.
B b How long _____?
A 5 days. I wanted to stay longer.
B c _____ spend a lot?
A Yes, it was quite expensive.
B d _____ any problems?
A Well, I lost all my money.
B e _____ do?
A I used my credit card to get more cash.

✓ **Check the answers**

Now you

9 What did you do yesterday? Use the words in brackets and write four true sentences – positive or negative.

a (watch TV) *I* _____
b (get up before 6:00 A.M.) *I* _____

c (speak English) **I** _____

d (eat meat) **I** _____

✓ **Check the answers**

19 Going to – for future plans (positive, negative and questions)

- She's going to buy a car
- What are you going to do?
- I'm not going to work

Meaning

1 Three people talk about their plans. Match the conversations to the plans.

Plans for retirement   **a**, **b** or **c**?
Plans for lottery money   **a**, **b** or **c**?
Plans for a [holiday/vacation] **a**, **b** or **c**?

---

a Fred Have you got any plans?

Peter Here's my list. Look – first **I'm going to buy** an expensive house in the Carribean, with ten bedrooms for all my family and friends. Then **I'm going to have** a big car – a Mercedes.

Fred And what about your job?

Peter My job!? Well, here's my decision – **I'm not going to work** another day!

---

b Andy So, you two, **what are you going to do**?

Sue Well, **we're not going to do** very much. **We're going to stay** in bed late every morning and then lie on the beach all day... and eat... and drink a lot.

Andy So , **you're going to have** a good time... And your cat?

Mike **It's going to have** a [holiday/vacation] with our [neighbour/neighbor]!

c Charles	So what about your parents – what are their plans?
Liz	Well, they both finish work next June. Then **they're going to move** to the country and live a quiet life with their two dogs.
Charles	And what about their London house? **Are they going to sell** it?
Liz	No, **they're not going to sell**. My sister, Jean – **she's going to stay** there.

✓ **Check the answers**

2 Answer the questions about *going* to in the conversations.

a In the conversations, **going to** is for decisions about the future. True/False?

b With **going to**, the speakers made the plans before the conversations. True/False?

c With **going to**, the speakers make the plans during the conversations. True/False?

✓ **Check the answers**

Form

3 Complete the tables using the conversations to help you. Use the words in the box.

's	'm	're	are	to	they	going	going	to	is

going to future

Positive & negative				
I	**a** *'m*			
He She It	**b** _____	(not)	going **d** _____	buy a car.
You We They	**c** _____			stay at home.

Questions				
e _____	you we **g** _____	**h** _____ to	buy a house?	
f _____	he she		have a [holiday/ vacation]?	
What	are is	you he **i** _____ **j** __ she	do? buy?	

 Check the answers

⚠Common mistakes

4 Correct the mistakes.

a I amn't going to watch TV tonight.
   I'm not going to watch TV tonight.
b She's going write a letter.

_____

c We going to fly to Paris on Saturday.

_____

d They not going to leave today.

_____

e Are going you to visit your parents?

_____

f What you going to do [at/on] the weekend?

_____

 Check the answers

Practice

5 Make four sentences using the words in the circle. You can use the words more than once.

> she   not   ?
> I   going   'm   to
> is   's   study

a *I'm going to study.*
b _____
c _____
d _____
e _____

✓ **Check the answers**

6 Write the words in the correct order.
a you to going are fly Paris to ?
   Are you going to fly to Paris?
b 're to going we eat breakfast

   _____

c they leave to going are now?

   _____

d n't he going school to to go is.

   _____

✓ **Check the answers**

7 Write about their plans.
Some sentences are negative.
a

He's going to watch TV.

b

She's _____

c

_____

d

_____

e

_____

f

_____

g

_____

 Check the answers

Now you

Write about some of your plans.

This weekend I'm _____

Next year _____

➢ Unit 11 *Present Progressive* for future arrangements

20 [*Have got/Have*] – for possession and availability (positive, negative and questions)

- She['s got/has] a new car
- New York [has got/has] a lot of [theatres/theaters]

Note: American English speakers don't use *have got* very often. They usually say *have*. The British use *have got*.

Meaning

1 Match the pictures with the texts below.

I **Max Thompson** [**has got/has**] 215 credit cards! But he **hasn't got** any money.

II **Have** you **got** a car? Yes, it's a very big car. The car [**has got/has**] 30 seats, a small golf course and a jacuzzi!

III The hotel [**has got/has**] a swimming pool and **it's got** a mini-bar in every room.

✓ **Check the answers**

2 Match the sentences with the meanings of *have got/has got*.

a He's got 215 credit cards.

b The car's got 30 seats.

c Have you got a car?

d The hotel's got a swimming pool.

Possessions

Availability

✓ Check the answers

Tip

[Have got/Have] is also for:

Illnesses	*I've got a headache/a cold.*
Family	*She's got three children/two sisters.*
Descriptions	*He's got brown hair/big ears.*

British English form

3 Complete the table. The texts on page 83 will help. Use the words in the box.

~~television~~	he	has	've	they

I We You **a** ____	have (n't) **b** ____			.
He She It	has (n't) 's	got	a swimming pool **c** a *television*	
Have	I we you they			?
d ____	**e** ____ she it			

✓ Check the answers

American English form

4 Complete the table with the words in the box.

swimming pool   she   do   you   has

I **a** ___ We They	have			.
He She It	**b** ___		**c** a ___ a television	
d ___	I we you they	have		?
Does	he **e** ___ it			

I We You They	don't	have	a television
He She It	doesn't		

⚠ Common mistakes

5 Put ☑ for a correct sentence and ☒ for an incorrect sentence.

a	She's got a new car.	☑	**b**	She've got a new car.	☒
c	Max have got a lot of credit cards.	☐	**d**	Max has got a lot of credit cards.	☐
e	The hotel's got a bar?	☐	**f**	Has the hotel got a bar?	☐
g	They've'n't got a house.	☐	**h**	They haven't got a house.	☐

i I no have a dog.   □   **j** I don't have a dog.   □

 Check the answers

Practice

6 Write sentences about Max, Jane and you. Use *have got/haven't got/has got/hasn't got*.

		Max	**Jane**	**you**
		✓	✗	?
		✗	✓	?
		✓	✓	?

a Max   *has got credit cards*   (*credit cards*)
b Jane_____   (*credit cards*)
c I_____   (*credit cards*)
d Max_____   (*a house*)
e Jane_____   (*a house*)
f I_____   (*a house*)
g Max and Jane _____   (*a car*)
h I_____   (*a car*)

 Check the answers

7 Make questions. Use the words in the box. Use the words more than once if necessary.

got	a	bar	the	hotel	has	you	camera	have
				Max	they			

a **Have they got a bar?**   e _____?
b _____? f _____?
c _____? g _____?
d _____? h _____?

✓ **Check the answers**

8 Complete the sentences with *has/doesn't have/have/don't have*.

a They love animals. They **have** two fish, five dogs and three cats.
b Jean walks to work. She _____ car.
c I can't pay. I _____ a credit card.
d Dave reads all the time. He _____ a lot of books.
e It's a great town. It _____ a library, a [theatre/theater] and a lot of restaurants.
f I want a long [holiday/vacation] but I _____ any money.
g We can't open the door. We _____ our keys.

✓ **Check the answers**

Now you

Write about possessions. Use *'ve got/haven't got/'s got/hasn't got*.

a **I've got** _____
b **My family** _____
c **I haven't got** _____
d **My friend** _____

Write about your village, town or city. Here are some words:

hospital   [cinema(s)/movie theater(s)]   hotel(s)   university

e **It's got** _____
f **It** _____
g **It hasn't got** _____
h **It** _____

First conditional
■ If it rains, I'll stay at home

Meaning

1 Find the answer to the questions in the texts.

a Both texts are about the future. True or False?
b Both texts are about Japan. True or False?

TV [Presenter/Anchor]   Mr. Dorritt, what do you think about the
                            future of our planet?
Jon Dorritt   It's very simple. The future is very simple. There are
                            two possibilities: we look after the planet or we
                            destroy the planet. Both are possible. **If we look after
                            the planet, we'll live. If we don't look after the
                            planet, we'll die.**

Millions of people live in Tokyo, Japan. It is very possible that more
people will live in Tokyo. **What will happen if there are more
people?** A Japanese architect wants one building in Tokyo for 300,000
people. It will be one mile high with 500 floors. It will take 15
minutes in the [lift/elevator] to go the 500th floor. It will be a city in
one building. It will have offices, [flats/apartments], restaurants,
[cinemas/movie theaters], banks, schools and hospitals. 'We won't
have enough space if there are more people,' says the architect. 'I
think it will be possible to find the money for the building. **If we get
the money, it will take 25 years to build the city.**'

✓ **Check the answers**

2 Look at the sentences in bold. They are in the *First Conditional*.

a Is the *First Conditional* about the present, the past, or the future?

b Is the *First Conditional* about something possible or impossible?

c Is the *First Conditional* about something possible or something certain?

Form

3 There are two parts in a sentence in the *First Conditional*.

a What tense is after **if** – the *Present Simple* or the *Future Simple* with **will**?

b What tense is in the other part – the *Present Simple* or the *Future Simple* with **will**?

c The **if** part is first - is there a comma (,)? Yes/No

d The **if** part is second – is there a comma (,)? Yes/No

4 Complete the table. Use the words in the box. The texts on page 88 will help.

> won't   ~~will~~   will   will

First conditional

If we look after the planet If we don't look after the planet,	we people	**a** *will* 'll	live die
If we find the money, If we don't find the money,	I he	**b** ____ **c** ____	start the building start the building
What **d** ____ happen if we don't look after the planet?			

 Check the answers

Common mistakes

5 Choose the correct sentence in each pair. One is correct ✓ one is incorrect ✗.

a If there will be more people, we will need more houses.

b If there are more people, we will need more houses.

c If we look after the planet, we live.
d If we look after the planet, we'll live.

e Will we have enough space if there are more people?
f Do we have enough space if there are more people?

✓ **Check the answers**

Tip

| **If or when?**
|
| *if* = it is possible
| *when* = it is certain
| **Ben** has a plane ticket for Egypt: '**When** I go to Egypt, I'll see the
| pyramids.'
| **Cliff** is choosing China or Egypt: '**If** I go to Egypt, I'll see the pyramids.'

Practice

6 Put *when* or *if*.
a   *If*   I'm late tonight...
b _____ I become president...
c _____ it gets dark tonight...
d _____ the film finishes...
e _____ the summer comes...
f _____ I win the race...

✓ **Check the answers**

7 Match the parts of the sentences.

a If I buy some eggs,   will you wash the dishes?
b Will you make a cake   there won't be anything to eat.
c If I cook dinner,   will you make an omelette?
d The cake will burn   if I buy the flour?
e If the cake burns,   if you bake it for 3 hours.

✓ **Check the answers**

8 Scientists are worried about the greenhouse effect. Put *if* or *will* in the blanks.

a *If* the planet gets warmer, the sea _____ get warmer.

b _____ the sea gets warmer, the ice at the North Pole _____ melt.

c What _____ happen _____ the North Pole melts? The sea _____ rise.

✓ **Check the answers**

9 Make sentences from the words in the circles.

a

> pass   you
> your   will   if   exams   you
> work   hard?

Will you pass your exams if you work hard?

b

> your
> if   exams,   pass   you
> college   to   go
> will   you

_____

c

> I   go
> to   I   history   college
> will   if   study

_____

Now you

Make true sentences about the future.

a I'll be surprised if...
b I'll be very happy if...
c If the weather is good tomorrow, I'll...
d If the weather is bad tomorrow,...

22

Present Perfect Simple – with *for/since* (positive, negative and question)
■ I've lived in Bangkok for three months
■ I've worked here since January

Meaning

1 Match the pictures to the texts about two jobs.

I
Bill started to study 'the knowledge' in1999. Now, two years later, he is still studying 'the knowledge'. 'The knowledge' is the information about all the streets in London. Bill wants to be a London taxi driver. In fact, **he's wanted to be a taxi driver since he was a boy**. 'Yes, there are a lot of streets in London!' he says. **'I've studied for two years** but there is a lot to learn.'

II

Nikki was a dancer. Then a friend gave her a pack of Tarot cards. She learned to read the cards very quickly. Now she is a Tarot reader in a shop called 'Mystery' in London. '**Have you been a Tarot reader for a long time?**' I asked Nikki. 'Oh, **I've worked here since January 2000**. I started 'Mystery' with two friends. **We've given Tarot readings here for three months** now. A lot of people come to ask about their relationships.'

✓ **Check the answers**

2 The tense in bold is the *Present Perfect Simple*.

a Is the *Present Perfect Simple* here about the past only, the present only or from past to present?

3 'I've studied for two years.'

a Is Bill studying now? Yes/No
b Did he start two years before? Yes/No
c Is the sentence about a past to present period? Yes/No

4 'I've worked here since January 2000.'

a Is Nikki working in the shop now? Yes/No
b Did she start in January 2000? Yes/No.

5 'He's wanted to be a taxi driver since he was a boy.'

a Does Bill want to be a taxi driver now? Yes/No.
b Did he want to be a taxi driver when he was a boy? Yes/No.

6 *for* and *since*

a Is *for* with a period of time or a starting time?
b Is *since* with a period of time or a starting time?

Form

7 Complete the table with the help of the texts on page 93. Use the words in the box.

for	have	~~'ve~~	since	's	worked

Positive and negative

I We You They	**a** *'ve*	(not)		**c** ____	**d** ____	three months two years a long time ten minutes
	have	(n't) (not)				
He She	**b** ____	(not)			**e** ____	January 5 o'clock he was a boy
It	has	(n't)				

Question

f ____	I we you they	studied	for four years ?
Has	he she it		since 1999 ?
How long have you studied?			

Response

Yes,	I we you they	have	No,	I we you they	haven't
	he she it	has		he she it	hasn't

 Check the answers

Past participle

We make the *Present Perfect Simple* with **have/has** (*I have*) + **past participle** (*worked*) of the verb.

With **regular** verbs the past participle is the same as the *Past Simple*.

Infinitive	Past Simple	Past participle
work	worked	worked
want	wanted	wanted
study	studied	studied

Irregular verbs are different.

Infinitive	Past Simple	Past participle
give	gave	given
be	was	been

More irregular verbs

8 Match the past participles in the box to the infinitive and *Past Simple* forms.

a do	→	did	→	***done***	
b drink	→	drank	→	_____	
c fly	→	flew	→	_____	
d go	→	went	→	_____	
e have	→	had	→	_____	
f leave	→	left	→	_____	
g run	→	ran	→	_____	
h see	→	saw	→	_____	
i spend	→	spent	→	_____	
j swim	→	swam	→	_____	
k take	→	took	→	_____	

had
gone
taken
~~done~~
flown
run
swum
drunk
seen
left
spent

 Check the answers

⚠ Common mistakes

9 Correct the mistakes. The mistakes are <u>underlined.</u>

a She <u>is</u> lived here for 3 weeks.
   She has/'s lived here for 3 weeks.

b <u>I felt</u> ill since 3 o'clock.

_____

c <u>They study</u> here for 2 months and they will go home tomorrow.

_____

d We've had this car <u>since</u> 4 years.

_____

e You've worked here <u>for</u> 1998.

_____

 Check the answers

Tip

Learn the question:
How long have you...?
... and add the past participle of a verb.
How long have you been a (+ job)?
How long have you lived in (+ place)?

Practice

10 Put the time expressions with _for_ or _since_.

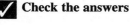

| ~~four days~~   a long time   [10 October/October 10] |
| I got up   10 seconds   Christmas   Tuesday   an hour |

for	**since**
four days	_____
_____	_____
_____	_____
_____	_____

 Check the answers

11 Draw lines to make sentences.

a I'velivedhereforthreeweeks.
 I've|lived|here|for|three|weeks.

b HowlonghaveEricandEricahadanewhouse?

c Mitchhasstudiedphysicssinceearlylastyear.

d Theyhaven'ttrieddietingforverylong.

e Howlonghassheeatennutsforbreakfast?

✓ **Check the answers**

12 Write a sentence in the *Present Perfect Simple* for the situations. Use *for* or *since*.

a She is in Beijing now. She arrived three days ago.
 She's been in Beijing for three days.

b They arrived in Bolivia on Thursday.
 They've been _____

c I know Jane. I met her three months ago.
 I've _____

d I have a laptop computer. I bought it in 1998.
 I _____

e I got divorced one year ago.
 I _____

f Rose studies economics now. She started two years ago.
 She _____

✓ **Check the answers**

13 Make questions with 'How long...?'

a Steve is in London now.
 How long *has he been in London?*

b Tina knows George.
 How long has she _____ ?

c Jean and Arthur are in Indonesia.
 How long have _____ ?

d Jane is married.
 How long _____ ?

e My uncle lives in Los Angeles.
 How _____ ?

f I have an old car.
 _____ ?

g I am divorced.

_____?

h Pete works in Honolulu.

_____?

i I know Robin.

_____?

j Louise is a teacher.

_____?

 Check the answers

Now you

Write true sentences about you and your family and friends.

a I've lived in _____ for _____
b I've studied _____ since _____
c My parents have lived in _____ since _____
d _____ has had the same job for _____
e I have _____ since I was very young.
f I haven't _____ to my best friend since _____

➤ Unit 23 *Present Perfect Simple* for indefinite past
➤ Unit 24 *Present Perfect Simple* and *Past Simple*
➤ Unit 25 *Present Perfect Progressive* with *for/since*

23 | *Present Perfect Simple – indefinite past (positive, negative and questions)*
■ I've been to Turkey

Meaning

1 Match the pictures to the texts.

a

b

wish you were here !!!

I

Dear [Mum/Mom] & Dad,

Having a great time here after one
week. *We've been* to the beach 5
times and *we've played* volleyball.
I've taken hundreds of photos. Went
to a museum yesterday because the
weather was bad. *We haven't sent*
a card to Doreen. *We've lost* her
address!
Love
Mary & Joe
xxxx

II

> **Have you ever eaten** a piece of glass or metal? Perhaps by accident.
> Well, Monsieur Mangeloup has a very interesting diet. He eats glass
> and metal – every day. **What has he eaten**? So far **he's eaten** 100
> wine bottles, 400 knives and forks, and 2 small aircraft! But **he hasn't
> tried** to eat the windows of his house.

✓ **Check the answers**

2 The <u>underlined</u> verbs are in the *Present Perfect Simple*.

a Are the verbs about the present, the past, or the future?
b Are the actions finished? Yes/No.
c Do we know the exact time of the actions? Yes/No.

✓ **Check the answers**

Form

**3 Complete the tables with the help of the texts on page 100. Use the
words in the box.**

| 's | ~~'ve~~ | has | ever | sent | been |

Present Perfect Simple

Positive and negative

I We You They	**a** *'ve* have	(n't) (not)	**c** _____ on the beach
He She It	**b** ____ has		**d** _____ a card

Question

Have	I we you they	**f** ___	been to Indonesia?
e ___	he she it		

Response

Yes,	I we you they	have	No,	I we you they	haven't
	he she it	has		he she it	hasn't

✓ **Check the answers**

Past participle

We make the *Present Perfect Simple* with **have/has** (*I have*) + **past participle** (*played*) of the verb.

With **regular** verbs the past participle is the same as the *Past Simple*.

Infinitive		**Past Simple**		**Past Participle**
play	→	played	→	played
try	→	tried	→	tried

Irregular verbs are different. Sometimes the *Past Simple* and past participle are the same...

lose	→	lost	→	lost
send	→	sent	→	sent

Sometimes they are different…

be	→	was	→	been
eat	→	ate	→	eaten

More irregular verbs

4 Match the past participles in the box to the infinitive and *Past Simple* forms.

a	break	→	broke	→	*broken*	had
b	win	→	won	→	_____	gone
c	fly	→	flew	→	_____	taken
d	go	→	went	→	_____	~~broken~~
e	have	→	had	→	_____	flown
f	meet	→	met	→	_____	run
g	run	→	ran	→	_____	swum
h	see	→	saw	→	_____	won
i	speak	→	spoke	→	_____	seen
j	swim	→	swam	→	_____	met
k	take	→	took	→	_____	spoken

✓ **Check the answers**

Practice

5 Paul, aged eight, asks his grandfather about his life. Make questions. Use the words in brackets.

a (be/Japan?) *Have you ever been to Japan?*   Yes, I have.

b (break/leg?) Have you ever br _____?   No, I haven't.

c (meet/famous person?) Have you ever _____?   No, I haven't.

d (always/live/in this house?) Have you _____?   Yes, I have.

e (speak/a king or queen?) Have _____?   No, I haven't.

f (win/a lot of money?) _____?   Yes, I have.

✓ **Check the answers**

6 Look at the grandfather's answers in exercise 5. Write sentences about the grandfather. Write true sentences about you.

Grandfather	You
a *He's been to Japan.* _____	**I**_____
b *He hasn't b* _____	**I**_____
c *He* _____	**I**_____
d _____	_____
e _____	_____
f _____	_____

 Check the answers

Tip

> No time given – use *Present Perfect Simple*
> Time given - use *Past Simple*
>
> Learn:
> She's been to Greece.
> She went to Greece last week.

△ Common mistakes

7 Correct the mistakes.

a Do you have been to Warsaw?
   Have you been to Warsaw?
b We not have been to Poland.

   _____

c He is been to Portugal.

   _____

d They has went home.

   _____

Check the answers

Now you

Write true sentences about you. Write about the past. Do not talk about the time or date. Use the *Present Perfect Simple*. Make two positive and two negative sentences.

Here are some verbs:

eat	be	drink	meet	see

a *I've* _____

b *I haven't* _____

c *I* _____

d _____

➤ Unit 22 *Present Perfect Simple* with *for/since*
➤ Unit 24 *Present Perfect Simple* and *Past Simple*
➤ Unit 25 *Present Perfect Progressive* with *for/since*

24 Present Perfect Simple and Past Simple
■ I've been to India
■ I went to India last year

Meaning

1 Match the titles to the three verses in the poem below.

a Languages
b Travel abroad
c Transport

I
I've been to France and **I've been** to Tangier
<u>I went</u> to Paris in May and to Tangier last year

II
Have you ever ridden a horse? **Have you learned** how to drive?
<u>I rode</u> across the Rockies last June, <u>I got</u> my driving licence in 1995

III
My sister speaks two languages, **she's learned** Spanish and **she's studied** Greek
<u>She left</u> for Spain at 2 o'clock and <u>she went</u> to Greece last week

---

 Check the answers

2 a What tense are the verbs in **bold**? *Present Perfect Simple/Past Simple*
  b What tense are the verbs <u>underlined?</u> *Present Perfect Simple/Past Simple*
  c What tense talks about the time or date? *Present Perfect Simple/Past Simple*
  d What tense doesn't talk about the time or date? *Present Perfect Simple/Past Simple*

Check the answers

Form

3 Complete the blanks with the words in the box.

> past participle   have   has

We make the *Present Perfect Simple* with **a** _____ or
b _____ and the **c** _____ of the verb.

4 Complete the blanks with the words in the box.

Positive	Negative	Question

> 've   have   has   learned   ridden   haven't   ~~hasn't~~

She's learned Greek.   She **a** *hasn't* learned   **b** ____ she **c** ____ Greek?
                       Greek.

I **d** ____ ridden a horse.   I **e** ____ ridden a   **f** ____ you **g** ____ a horse?
                               horse.

5 Complete the table.

Infinitive	Past Simple	Past participle
Regular Verbs		
learn	**a** *learned*	learned
study	studied	**b** _____
Irregular Verbs		
leave	left	**c** _____
go	**d** _____	gone
ride	**e** _____	**f** _____
get	**g** _____	[got/gotten]
be	**h** _____	been

✓ **Check the answers**

Tip

No time given – use *Present Perfect Simple*
Time given – use *Past Simple*

Learn:
She's been to Greece.
She went to Greece last week.

Common mistakes

6 Which is correct? In each pair, one sentence is correct ✓ and one sentence is incorrect ✗.

a He went to Thailand three years ago. ✓
b He's been to Thailand three years ago. ✗

c What did you do last week?
d What have you done last week?

e I saw the Rolling Stones in 2000.
f I've seen the Rolling Stones in 2000.

g Mary has wrote a lot of books.
h Mary has written a lot of books.

i Did they live in Paris 5 years ago?
j Have they lived in Paris 5 years ago?

k When has he arrived?
l When did he arrive?

✓ **Check the answers**

Practice

7 Make sentences from the words in the circles.
a

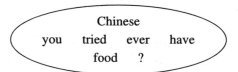

Have you ever tried Chinese food?
b

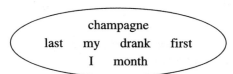

c

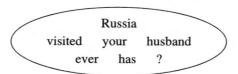

Russia
visited   your   husband
ever   has   ?

---

d

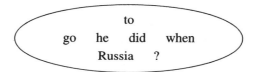

to
go   he   did   when
Russia   ?

 Check the answers

8 Complete the blanks with the *Present Perfect Simple* or the *Past Simple*. Use the words in brackets.

a I *played* (play) tennis yesterday afternoon.
b _____ (you/play) tennis before?
c I _____ (play) once when I was 15.
d When I was a teenager, I _____ (not/like) [sport/sports].
e _____ (you/see) a tag wrestling match?
f I _____ (see) wrestling on TV.
g I _____ (go) to a match when I was in Los Angeles last year.

 Check the answers

9 Here is an interview with Geoffrey Tarcher, a writer. Fill in the blanks with the *Past Simple* or the *Present Perfect Simple*. Use the verb: *write – wrote – written*.

Interviewer	How many books a ***have you written***?
Geoffrey	Oh, about 30.
Interviewer	When **b** _____ the first book?
Geoffrey	I **c** _____ it in 1985.
Interviewer	**d** _____ any short stories?
Geoffrey	Yes, I **e** _____ a collection of short stories two years ago.

 Check the answers

Now you

Write about something you have done (*Present Perfect Simple*). Then write about when you did it (*Past Simple*).

a *I've* _____

   I _____

b *I've* _____

   I _____

> Unit 22 *Present Perfect Simple* with *for/since*
> Unit 23 *Present Perfect Simple* for the indefinite past
> Unit 25 *Present Perfect Progressive* with *for/since*

25 Present Perfect Progressive with *for/since* (positive, negative and questions)

■ I've been working all day

Meaning

1 a Which text is about driving a taxi? I or II?

b Which text is about driving tests? I or II?

I

Charles takes his test again tomorrow. It's the 52nd time. **He's been taking** the test for 35 years. **He's been hoping** to pass it since he was 25. As a 60-year-old he has had 1,200 driving lessons. Good luck tomorrow, Charles!

II

Sarah, a reporter, has an interview with Jean. Jean is a female taxi driver in London.

Sarah   **How long have you been driving** around the streets of London?

Jean   For about 5 years. But **I haven't been driving** a black taxi for 5 years. I drove around London for 2 years in my own car. **I've been living** in South London since I was a girl.

Sarah   What's the biggest tip you've ever had?

Jean   A customer gave me £200 last year... I'm sure it was a mistake. The fare was only £35!

 Check the answers

2 **a** What tense is **in bold**? The *Past Simple,* the *Present Perfect Simple*
   or the *Present Perfect Progressive?*

   b Is the tense **in bold** for situations from the past to the present?
   Yes/No

3 **'He's been taking the test for 35 years.'**

a When did he start the driving tests?

b Is he taking tests now?

4 *for* and *since*

a Is *for* with a period of time or a starting time?

b Is *since* with a period of time or a starting time?

✓ **Check the answers**

Form

**5 Complete the table with the help of the texts on page 111. Use the
words in the box.**

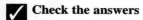

| 's | ~~'ve~~ | has | working | been | since |

Present Perfect Progressive

I We You They	**a** *'ve* have	(n't) (not)				
He She It	**b** _____ has		**d** ____	**e** _____ here	for 10 years **f** ____ 2000	
Have	I you we they					
c ____ he she it						?

Response

Yes,	I we you they	have	No,	I we you they	haven't
	he she it	has		he she it	hasn't

 Check the answers

Tip

Don't use the *Present Perfect Progressive* with *have* when it means 'own'.

~~I've been having a car for two years~~. → I've had a car for two years.

Don't use the *Present Perfect Progressive* with *know*.

~~I've been knowing my best friend since I was a teenager.~~ → I've known my best friend since I was a teenager.

⚠ Common mistakes

6 Correct the mistakes.

a How long you have been learning English?
   How long have you been learning English?

b She's living in Bangkok since 1988.

_____

c We study in New York since January.

_____

 Check the answers

Practice

7 Make questions with *How long...?* and the *Present Perfect Progressive*.

a Andy is learning Thai.
How long has he been *learning Thai*?

b I work in Istanbul.
How long have you _____?

c Mike and Sally are training for the Boston Marathon.
How long have _____?

d Emma is waiting for a bus.
How long _____?

e My wife and I are talking on the phone.
How _____?

f Tricia is reading the newspaper.
_____?

✔ **Check the answers**

8 Put the time expressions with *for* or *since*.

| ~~four days~~   a long time   last summer   I arrived |
| 10 minutes   1999   Monday   3 weeks |

for	since
four days	————
————	————
————	————
————	————

✔ **Check the answers**

9 Write sentences for the situations. Use the *Present Perfect Progressive*.

a I'm waiting for a train. I started waiting 20 minutes ago. I've been waiting for the train *for 20 minutes*.

b Jean is looking for a new house. She started 2 weeks ago. She's been

  c David and Allison dance together. They started last December. They've

  _____

  d My sister and I started jobs with the same company – NuBooks - in the
     summer. We _____

  e Bruce started writing a letter at 3 o'clock. _____

✓ **Check the answers**

Now you

Write true sentences about you and your family and friends. Use the
***Present Perfect Progressive*.**

  a I've been living in _____ for _____
  b I've been studying _____ since _____
  c My parents have been living in _____ since _____
  d _____ has been working in the the same job for _____
  e I have _____ since I was a child.

> ➤ Unit 22 *Present Perfect Simple* with *for/since*
> ➤ Unit 23 *Present Perfect Simple* for the indefinite past
> ➤ Unit 24 *Present Perfect Simple* and *Past Simple*

26 | *Past Simple* and *used to*
■ I used to smoke
■ I smoked one cigarette last year

Meaning

1 Find the answer to the question in the text below.

Is the text about the 1960s or the 1920s?

A Tell me about the 19_ _s...

B Well, **we used to wear** miniskirts – me too, I don't now! **The boys used to have** hairstyles like the Beatles. Once I got tickets for a Beatles concert in Liverpool. I went all the way from London to Liverpool with a friend to see them. I was a student and we wanted to change the world. 'Make Love not War,' we said. **I used to go** on marches to ban the bomb. A lot of people smoked drugs then. **I didn't use to smoke** cigarettes or drugs! **What did you use to do** then?

✓ **Check the answer**

2 Look at *used to* in bold in the text.

a Is *used to* about now or the past?

b Is *used to* about one action or repeated actions?

3 'We used to wear miniskirts.'

a Did they wear miniskirts in the past?

b Did they wear miniskirts one time or many times?

c Do they wear miniskirts now?

✓ **Check the answers**

Form

4 Complete the table with the help of the text on page 116. Use the words in the box.

~~use~~	used	didn't

I He She It We You They	**a** ____ to		work. wear miniskirts.
	b ____	**c** *use* to	
Did	I she	use to	work? wear miniskirts?

 Check the answers

Practice

5 Make sentences from the words in the circles.

a

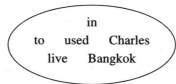

in
to   used   Charles
live   Bangkok

Charles used to live in Bangkok.

b

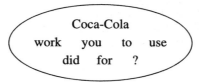

Coca-Cola
work   you   to   use
did   for   ?

c

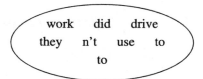

work   did   drive
they   n't   use   to
to

d

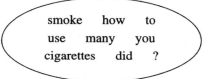

smoke   how   to
use   many   you
cigarettes   did   ?

 Check the answers

Tip

> *Used to* is for repeated actions.
> If there was only one action, use the *Past Simple*.
> ~~We used to go to a Beatles concert in 1965.~~
> → We went to a Beatles concert in 1965.

⚠ Common mistakes

6 Correct the mistakes.

a She use to smoke a lot.   *She used to smoke a lot.*

b Did he used to smoke?   _____

c They didn't used to smoke.   _____

d I used to smoking.   _____

e We used smoke all the time.   _____

 Check the answers

7 Match a sentence from A with a sentence from B. Complete the sentence in B with *used to*.

A	B
a I had a small dog when I was 9,	_____ walk everywhere.
b We didn't have a car.	_____ go camping in Spain.
c We had great [holidays/vacations]	_____ work in a big office.
d My father was a pilot.	_____ study very hard.
e My mother was a secretary.	*I used to* take it for a walk every day.
f My sister went to [university/college].	_____ fly from Heathrow airport.

✓ **Check the answers**

8 Complete the sentences with *used to/didn't use to* and a verb from the box.

~~eat~~   eat   read   drink   live   play   ride   be

a Peter became a vegetarian two years ago. He *used to eat* a lot of meat.
b Peter _____ a bicycle but he sold it last year.
c He eats a lot now but when he was young he _____ very much.
d Andy _____ Peter's best friend but he isn't now.
e Andy _____ in San Antonio but he lives in Austin now.
f Peter _____ the piano but he hates music now.
g Peter often reads newspapers but he _____ them.
h Peter _____ a lot of coffee but now he only likes tea.

Now you

Write true sentences about your past life.

a I used to _____ but I don't now.
b I didn't use to _____ but I do now.

> ➤ Unit 16 *Past Simple* regular verbs
> ➤ Unit 17 *Past Simple* regular and irregular verbs
> ➤ Unit 18 *Past Simple* (negative and questions)

27 | *Past Progressive* and *Past Simple*
■ I was working
■ I worked

Meaning

1 Read the true story about Henry Bourse in Australia. Find the answer to the question in the text below. How many sharks have attacked Henry Bourse? One, two, or three?

> Henry Bourse **was working** near Melbourne, in Australia. A shark <u>attacked</u> him when he **was filming** underwater. The shark bit his leg and swam away with it.
>
> Henry wasn't worried because the leg was plastic. A different shark bit off the same leg 5 years before!

 Check the answer

2 Answer the questions about the grammar.

a What tense is **in bold**? *Past Simple* or *Past Progressive*?
b What tense is <u>underlined</u>? *Past Simple* or *Past Progressive*?
c Which action was in progress first – 'film' or 'attack'?
d Look at the diagram below. Which action is 'film'? 1 or 2?
e Which action is 'attack'? 1 or 2?

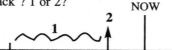

f 'He was filming' – does this describe the middle of an action or a finished action?
g 'A shark attacked him' – does this describe the middle of an action or a finished action?

 Check the answers

Form

3 Complete the table. Use the words in the box.

| were | ~~was~~ | were | was | n't | not |

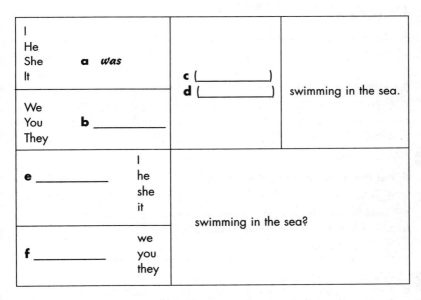

I He She **a** *was* It	**c** (_____) **d** (_____)	swimming in the sea.
We You **b** _____ They		

e _____	I he she it	swimming in the sea?
f _____	we you they	

⚠ Common mistakes

4 Correct the mistakes. There is a mistake <u>underlined</u> in each sentence.

a <u>You was reading</u> when I saw you.
   You were reading when I saw you.
b I met him when <u>I shopping</u> in Sydney.
   _____
c When I woke up, the morning was wonderful – <u>the sun shone</u>.
   _____
d <u>I read</u> when you phoned him.
   _____
e <u>You was sleep</u> when I phoned.
   _____

Tip

With the *Simple Past*
The action is last.

Practice

5 Match the parts of the sentences to make four true stories.

a The *Titanic* was crossing the Atlantic,   John Lennon was walking to
                                                      his New York apartment.
b When he was shot   when a gunman shot him.
c President Kennedy was   when Neil Armstrong
   travelling in a limousine in Texas   walked on the moon.
d The world was watching   when it hit an iceberg.

 Check the answers

6 Put the words in the correct order.

a the police/was/when/a thief/in a house in Paris/sleeping/arrived.
   A thief was sleeping in a house in Paris when the police arrived.

b across/I/running/the road/a car/me/hit/was/when.

_____

c flying/were/they/when/to Australia/crashed/the plane

_____

d not/listening/we/when/the teacher/the homework/gave/were

_____

e doing/what/you/when/Princess Diana/were/you heard/the news about/?

_____

f you/was/when/snoring/I/came in/?

_____

g n't/when/raining/I/it/arrived/was

_____

h the phone/was/I/rang/reading/when

_____

 Check the answers

7 Fill in the blanks in the true story. Put the verb in brackets in the *Past Simple* **or the** *Past Progressive.*

In 1981 in Baku, on the Caspian Sea, a thief **a** *was breaking* (break) into an empty [flat/apartment] when suddenly he **b** _____ (feel) very tired. He **c** _____ (have) a hot bath and then **d** _____ (drink) some glasses of vodka. When he **e** _____ (drink) the vodka, he **f** _____ (see) a piano in the [flat/apartment]. He **g** _____ (start) playing the piano and singing. The [neighbours/neighbors] **h** _____ (phone) the police because of the noise. When the police **i** _____ (arrive), the thief **j** _____ (sing).

 Check the answers

Now you

Think of two well-known events, for example, when Princess Diana died, Kennedy was shot, and write what you were doing at the time.

a *When* _____ *I was* _____

b *When* _____

➤ Unit 15 *Past Simple – there was/there were*
➤ Unit 16 *Past Simple* – regular verbs
➤ Unit 17 *Past Simple* – regular and irregular verbs
➤ Unit 18 *Past Simple* – (negative and questions)

28 | *Will* for predictions, decisions made now and offers
- It will rain
- I'll answer the phone
- I'll help you

Meaning

1 Match the pictures to the situations below.

a

b

c

I

> [At/On] the weekend **it will rain. There will be** some sun on Saturday afternoon but **there won't be** any sunshine on Sunday.

II

> It's OK, Dave. **I'll answer** it.

III

> That looks heavy. **I'll carry** it for you.

 Check the answers

2 Look at *will* in bold in the texts above. Match the examples with the meanings.

a ...it will rain   prediction
b There will be some sun...   decisions made now
c There won't be any sunshine...   offer to help
d I'll answer it.   prediction
e I'll carry it.   prediction

 Check the answers

Tip

> Don't use the *Present Simple* for new decisions.
> I~~ answer it~~.   I'll answer it.
> I~~ go now~~.   I'll go now.
> Don't use *I will* for decisions made now. Use *I'll*.
> ~~I will answer it~~.   I'll answer it.
> Don't use *I'll* for old decisions.
> What are your plans? ~~I'll leave tomorrow~~. I'm going to leave tomorrow.

Form

3 Complete the table. Use the words in the box.

'll	will	~~arrive~~

He She It We You They	'll **a** _____ won't	**c *arrive*** late. win.
I	**b** _____	answer the phone. carry your bag.

 Check the answers

⚠ Common mistakes

4 Correct the mistakes. The mistakes are <u>underlined</u>.

a I think the train <u>will to be</u> late.
I think the train will be late.

b <u>I phone</u> you tomorrow morning, OK?

_____

c **A**: I've lost all my money. **B**: <u>I lend</u> you some some money.

_____

d That's the phone. <u>I answer</u> it.

_____

e The weather <u>not will be</u> hot tomorrow.

_____

✓ **Check the answers**

Practice

5 Complete the sentences. Use *I'll* and the correct verb from the box.

~~send~~ stay cook go help drive

a 'Have a good time in Tokyo.' 'Thanks, *I'll send* you a postcard.'
b 'You look tired.' 'Really? I think _____ to bed now.'
c 'I'm very, very hungry.' 'Really? _____ something for you to eat.'
d 'Look at all these dirty dishes!' 'Don't worry, _____ you with it.'
e 'Would you like to [come out/go] with me now?' 'No, I'm too tired. _____ here.'
f 'I'm late for my train.' 'Don't worry, _____ you to the station.'

✓ **Check the answers**

6 Match the predictions.

What are your predictions for next year?
a I think the weather around the world will   be more tourists in London.
b I think the stock market will   win a gold medal.
c I think the dollar will   be very wet.
d I think the British runner will   be strong.
e I think there will   crash.

✓ **Check the answers**

Now you

Make two predictions about two people in your family.

a *I think* _____

b *I think* _____

29 | I'd like.../Would you like...? for requests, offers and invitations
- Would you like coffee?
- I'd like an orange juice

Meaning

1 Find the answer to the question in the dialogue below.

A customer goes into a bank to exchange British sterling. What currency does she get?

Customer	**I'd like to exchange** sterling for Euros, please.
Clerk	Euros, [madam/ma'am]?
Customer	Yes, please.
Clerk	Certainly, [madam/ma'am]. Err, we don't have Euros, I'm afraid. **Would you like to have Swiss francs?**
Customer	No, thank you.
Clerk	What about yen ? **Would you like** Japanese yen?
Customer	No, thank you. **I'd like Euros**.
Clerk	U.S. dollars?
Customer	No, thank you.
Clerk	Roubles?
Customer	No, thank you.
Clerk	Indian rupees?
Customer	No...

 Check the answer

2 Look at the language in bold in the dialogue above and answer the questions.

a 'I'd like to...' is a request. True/False?

b 'I'd like...' is a request. True/False?
c 'I'd like...'/'I'd like to...' mean now or in general?
d 'I'd like to...'/'I'd like... mean 'I want now' True/False?
e 'Would you like to...?' is an offer. True/False?
f 'Would you like....?' is an offer. True/False?
g 'Would you like...?'/'Would you like to...?' mean now or in general?
h 'Would you like...?'/'Would you like to...?' mean 'Do you want now?' True/ False?

✔ **Check the answers**

Form

3 Are they possible? Look at the dialogue above.

a *I'd like to* + verb   Yes/No?
b *I'd like* + noun   Yes/No?
c *Would you like to* + verb   Yes/No?
d *Would you like* + noun   Yes/No?
e *I'd like have*   Yes/No?
f *Would you like have*   Yes/No?

✔ **Check the answers**

4 Complete the table. Use the words in the box.

| to   would   ~~'d~~ |

I **a** *'d* like	a coffee Swiss francs to have coffee **c** ___ eat lunch		
b _____ you like		?	Yes, please. No, thank you.
What would you like?			Tea, please.

✔ **Check the answers**

Tip

I'd like coffee = now
I like coffee = in general, always

Would you like coffee? = now
Do you like coffee? = in general, always

⚠ Common mistakes

5 Correct the mistakes.

a Do you like any orange juice now, sir?
   Would you like any orange juice now, sir?

b You like your coffee now, [madam/ma'am]?

_____

c I'd like order steak and [chips/fries], please.

_____

d Would you like have the bill, sir?

_____

e I like a beer, please.

_____

✔ Check the answers

Practice

6 Make offers. Use *Would you like...?*

a

b

Would you like (some) pizza?   Would you like_____?

c

d

Would you_____?   Would_____?

e  f

_____ ?   _____ ?

✓ **Check the answers**

7 Make offers and invitations. Draw lines (|) to make sentences.

a Would|you|like|to|go|to|the|party?
b Wouldyouliketoeatnow?
c Wouldyouliketogoforawalk?
d Wouldyouliketogowithmetotheconcert?
e WouldyouliketomeetDianaandmeattherestaurant?

✓ **Check the answers**

8 Make offers and requests. Use *Would you like to ...?*

a play/tennis/tomorrow   ***Would you like to play tennis tomorrow?***
b go/dancing   Would you like to _____?
c go/out/with/me   Would you like _____?
d go/to/the/party   Would you _____?
e go/for/a/drive   Would _____?
f go/to/a/concert   _____?
g go/out/for/a/drink   _____?

✓ **Check the answers**

9 Choose the correct form.

a *'Do you like* a coffee?/*Would you like* a coffee?' 'Yes, please.'
  'Would you like a coffee?'* is correct.
b *'What do you like/What would you like* to eat?' 'Pizza, please.'
c *'Do you like/Would you like* something to drink?' 'No, thank you.'
d *'I like/I'd like* bananas but I never eat them.'
e *'Do you like/Would you like* a Coke?' 'Yes, please.'
f *'Do you like/Would you like?'* 'I prefer warm drinks, actually.'

✓ **Check the answers**

Now you

You're in a restaurant. Offer your friend a drink and something to eat.

a *Would you* _____?
b *Would* _____?

The waiter asks you for your order.

a *I'd* _____
b *And I* _____

30 Can...?/Could...?/[Is it all right if...?/May...?] for requests and permission

- Can I borrow your dictionary?
- Can you help me?
- [Is it all right if/May] I go now?

Meaning

1 Match the situations with the dialogues below.

a Talking to a friend on the train
b Talking to another student in the classroom
c Talking to another student in the classroom
d Talking to a friend at home at the table
e Talking to a friend in the kitchen

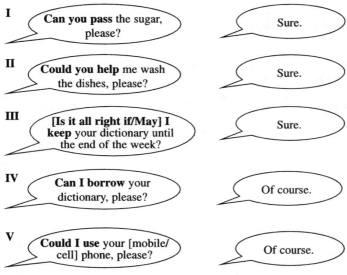

I Can you pass the sugar, please? — Sure.

II Could you help me wash the dishes, please? — Sure.

III [Is it all right if/May] I keep your dictionary until the end of the week? — Sure.

IV Can I borrow your dictionary, please? — Of course.

V Could I use your [mobile/cell] phone, please? — Of course.

 Check the answers

2 Are they requests or asking for permission?

a *Can I...?*   request/ask for permission?
b *Could I...?*   request/ask for permission?
c *Can you...?*   request/ask for permission?
d *Could you...?*   request/ask for permission?
e *[Is it all right if/may] I...?* request/ask for permission?

3 Match the forms and the meanings

a *[Is it all right if/may]...*   is for a small request
b *Can...*   is for a big request
c *Could...*   is for a bigger request

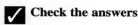 **Check the answers**

Form

4 Complete the table. Use the words in the box.

if   sure   you   I

Asking for permission		
Can I Could **a** _____ Is it all right **b** _____ I	use the phone? borrow your dictionary?	**d** _____. Of course.
Requests		
Can **c** _____ Could you	pass the sugar to me? help me?	

 Check the answers

⚠ Common mistakes

5 Correct the mistakes.

a Can I to have your phone number?
    Can I have your phone number?
b It is all right to send you an e-mail?

c You could help me with my homework?

_____

d Could I to leave early, please?

_____

✓ **Check the answers**

Practice

6 Match the questions to the answers.

a Could I use your [mobile/cell] phone?

b [Is it all right if/May] I stay with Jim tonight?

c Can you pass me the milk?

d Can I read your newspaper?

e Could you help me with my French homework?

OK, but when are you going to come home?

OK, but I only studied it for one year at school.

Sorry, it's not working.

Of course, here you are.

Sure, but it's yesterday's.

✓ **Check the answers**

7 What do you say? Use *Can I...? Can you...? Could I...? Could you...? [Is it all right if/May] I...?*

a You want to use my phone.
   Can I use your phone?/Could I use your phone?/ [Is it all right if/May] I use your phone?

b You want to borrow my pen.
   Can _____

c You are hot. The window is shut. I am near the window.
   Could _____

d You want to change the channel on the TV.
   Is _____

e You want my address.

   _____

f You are on the phone. You want to speak to Charlie.

   _____

✓ **Check the answers**

Now you

a Write one request. Think of a person and write a request to him or her.

_____

b Ask for permission. Think of a person and ask them for permission.

_____

➤ Unit 31 *can/can't/could/couldn't* for ability

31 | *Can.../can't.../could/ couldn't* for ability

- I can swim
- He can't drive
- I could read when I was six

Meaning

1 Match the pictures with the texts below.

a

b

c

d

I   These men **can** fly. They say that if $\sqrt{1\%}$ of the people in the world fly together in a group, there will be world peace.

II   This machine **couldn't** fly!

III   This bird **could** fly when it was three days old.

IV   This bird **can't** fly now!

✓ **Check the answers**

2 Answer questions about *can* in the texts above.

a *can/can't* = it is possible to/it is not possible to. True or False?
b *could/couldn't* = it was possible to/it was not possible to. True/False?
c Is *can* for the past, the present or the future?
d Is *could* for the past, the present or the future?

 Check the answers

Tip

There is no *to* after *can*:
I can ~~to~~ speak English.

Form

3 Complete the table. Use the words in the box.

~~can~~   swim   can't   could

I He She It We You They	**a** *can* **b** _____ could couldn't	**d** _____ fly
Can **c** _____	I he she it we you they	fly?

Yes,	I he she it	can. could.
No,	we you they	can't. couldn't.

Can't is short for **cannot**. **Can't** is for informal written and spoken English.

 Check the answers

Common mistakes

4 Correct the mistakes.

a I can to swim.
   I can swim.

b She cans speak French.

_____

c Do you can drive?

_____

d They not could ski.

_____

e We could to read when we were three.

_____

 Check the answers

Practice

5 Correct the information if necessary. Sometimes the information is correct.

a Cats can't see at night. ✗
   Cats can see at night.

b Parrots can talk. ✓

_____

c Penguins can fly.

_____

d Dogs can climb trees.

　　_____

e Some Swiss people can speak Italian.

　　_____

f Kangaroos can't jump.

　　_____

✓ **Check the answers**

6 Paula and Andy

Paula	✔	✔	✘
Andy	✘	✔	✔

Ask questions about Paula and Andy. Make questions for the answers. Use the verbs in the box.

> ride　　play　　drive

a *Can Paula play the piano?*　　Yes, she can. She's very musical.
b *Can Andy* _____?　Yes, he can. [He's got/He has] a big
　　　　　　　　　　　　　　　　Honda.
c _____?　No, she can't. And she can't drive a car.
d _____?　No, he can't. He isn't very musical.
e _____?　Yes, she can. She likes to ride very fast.
f _____?　Yes, he can. That's his job.

7 Write sentences about Paula and Andy.

a Paula can play *the piano*.
b Paula can _____
c She _____
d Andy can ride _____
e Andy can't_____
f He _____
g They _____

✓ **Check the answers**

8 Complete the sentences with *can, can't, could, couldn't* and one of the verbs in the box.

~~understand~~   have   read   hear   see   see

a I don't speak Japanese so I ***couldn't understand*** Yoko last night.
b I lost my glasses so I _____ very well yesterday.
c Pierre and I speak English. Now we _____ a conversation.
d You are speaking very quietly. I _____ you.
e My house is on a hill. You _____ for miles.
f I did well at school. I _____ when I was five.

Now you

Write about two things you can do and two things you can't do.

a *I can* _____
b *I* _____
c *I can't* _____
d _____

Write about two things you could do when you were seven and two things you couldn't do.

a *I could* _____*when I was seven.*
b *I* _____
c *I couldn't* _____*when I was seven.*
d *I* _____

➤ Unit 30 *can.../could.../[is it all right if/may]...?* for requests and permission

32 | *Might* – for possibility
■ It might rain

Meaning

1 Match the pictures and the conversations.

a   b

I Be careful! You **might** fall…   I'm OK, [Mum/Mom]

II Oh, no… We **might** miss the train.   It's OK. We have 30 minutes.

III Look! It **might** rain.   Perhaps.

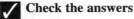 **Check the answers**

2 Answer the questions about *might* in the conversations above.

a Is *might* for the present, past or future?

b Does *might* mean something is certain or possible?

c Does *might* mean *'will perhaps'*?

d Does *might not* mean *'perhaps will not'*?

e Does *might* mean a big chance or a small chance something will happen?

✓ **Check the answers**

Tip

No *s* with *might*:
She mights be late.

Use *not* for the negative:
He might not be late.

Form

3 Complete the table. Use the words in the box.

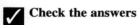

arrive   fall   might

I He She It We You They	**a** ———— (not)	**b** _____ . **c** *arrive* late.

✓ **Check the answers**

⚠ Common mistakes

4 Correct the mistakes.

a The train mights be late.
The train might be late.

b It might to rain.

_____

c They not might like the film.

_____

d Jean mights not pass her exam.

_____

 Check the answers

Practice

5 Match the sentences.

a Peter might not come.	It's our day off.
b I might not sleep tonight.	There's a great new film [on/playing].
c We might stay in bed tomorrow.	It's really late now.
d They might go to the [cinema/movies].	I ate too much.

Check the answers

6 Use the pictures to write about possible situations.

a *It might rain.*   **b** *It might not rain.*

c I might watch _____   **d** He might _____

e She _____   **f** He _____

g We _____   **h** _____

i _____

✓ **Check the answers**

Now you

Write about your *possible* plans for tomorrow. Use *might*. Here are some verbs:

watch TV	play tennis	get up early	send an e-mail

a *I might* _____
b *I* _____
c _____

33 | *Shall* – for suggestions and offers
■ Shall we leave now?
■ Shall I carry your bag?

Note: American English speakers don't use *shall* very often.

Meaning

1 Match the pictures to the conversations below.

a   b

I

What do you think? **Shall I** buy it or not?

Well, I like the [colour/color].

Do you think it's too small?

No, it's perfect for you.

II

Shall we buy it?

Well, I like the [colour/color].

Do you think it's too small?

No, there are only two of us.

✓ **Check the answers**

2 Answer the questions about *Shall I?* and *Shall we?* in the conversations above.

a *Shall I?* and *Shall we?* ask for an opinion. True or False?

b *Shall I?* and *Shall we?* mean 'Is it a good idea?'. True or False?

c *Shall I?* and *Shall we?* are about the present, the past or the future.

3 Match the sentences to the meanings.

a Shall I carry your bag?

b Shall we go to the park?   Offer

c Shall I help you with your homework?   Suggestion

d Shall we watch TV now?

✓ **Check the answers**

Tip

Look at the difference between the two questions.
Shall I drive?   = Is it a good idea for **me** to drive?
Will you drive? = I ask **you** to drive.

Form

4 Complete the table. Use the words in the box.

| ~~we~~   I   shall   go |

a Shall	b *we*	help you?
	c *go*	d *I* now?

✓ **Check the answers**

⚠ Common mistakes

5 Correct the mistakes.

a Shall we to go?
   Shall we go?

b Shall I opening the window?
   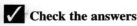

c Shall I to answer the phone?

Shall I answer the phone (handwritten)

d We shall leave now?

Shall we leave now (handwritten)

✓ **Check the answers**

6 Make sentences with *Shall I?* Use words from box A and box B in each sentence.

A

~~answer~~	pay
carry	make	drink
open	go

B

~~it~~	for the book	it for you
it	the window	some tea
	to the supermarket	

a That's the phone.   *Shall I answer it?*
b My suitcase is very heavy.   _____
c I'm thirsty.   _____
d I left my credit card at home. _____
e It's hot in here.   _____
f I don't want this Coke.   _____
g There's no milk.   _____

✓ **Check the answers**

7 What do you say? Use *Shall I?* or *Shall we?*

a You want to call your friend later. What do you say to her?
   Shall I call you later?
b You are not sure whether to buy the black jeans. Ask your friend.
   Shall I _____
c You want to go with your friend to the [cinema/movies]. Make a suggestion.
   Shall _____
d You want to go to Tokyo with your friend. Make a suggestion.

   _____

e You want to take your car but you're not sure. Ask your friend.

   _____

f It's dark in the room. Offer to turn the light on.

   _____

✓ **Check the answers**

Now you

Write two offers you can make to a friend or someone in your family.

a *Shall I*_____

b _____

Write two suggestions you can make to a friend or someone in your family.

c *Shall we* _____

d _____

34 | *Must/mustn't* – for obligation and prohibition
■ I must go
■ You mustn't sit there

Note: *Must* and *musn't* are rarely used in spoken contemporary American English.

Meaning

1 Match the situations to the texts below.
a Advice in a fitness magazine.
b A mother talks to her teenage daughter.
c Someone on the way to the airport.
d Someone wants a job.

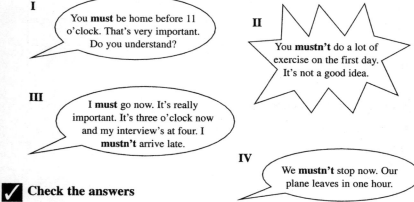

I You **must** be home before 11 o'clock. That's very important. Do you understand?

II You **mustn't** do a lot of exercise on the first day. It's not a good idea.

III I **must** go now. It's really important. It's three o'clock now and my interview's at four. I **mustn't** arrive late.

IV We **mustn't** stop now. Our plane leaves in one hour.

✓ Check the answers

2 Answer the questions about *must* in the texts above.

a *Must* is for the future and the present. True or False?
b *Mustn't* is for the future and the present. True or False?
c *Must* is for something necessary. True or False?
d *Must* is for when the speaker thinks something is very important. True or False?

e *Mustn't* is for a bad idea. True or False?

f *Mustn't* is for when the speaker thinks something is bad. True or False?

 Check the answers

Tip

There is no *to* after *must*:
I must ~~to~~ go.

Form

3 Complete the table. Use the words in the box.

~~must~~	go	late	mustn't

I He She It We You They	**a** *must* **b** _____	**c** _____ now. be **d** _____

 Check the answers

⚠Common mistakes

4 Correct the mistakes.

a You must to wait.
You must wait.

b I not must stay.

_____

c They mustn't to go.

_____

d She musts go home.

_____

e We not must eat so much.

_____

☑ **Check the answers**

Practice

5 Match the sentences.

a He's a very nice person. —————— I must go shopping.
b My friends are coming to dinner. We must be patient.
c The bus is 30 minutes late. She must go to the post office.
d She needs stamps. You must meet him.

☑ **Check the answers**

6 Complete the sentences. Use _must_ or _mustn't_ and a verb from the box.

~~go~~	see	leave	win	forget
hurry	clean	worry	be	phone/call

a I _must go_ to the bank. I've only got 1000 yen in my pocket.
b Our train leaves in 15 minutes. We _____
c It's a wonderful film. You _____ it.
d The bus leaves in 10 minutes. I _____ late.
e Charlie is waiting for a call. I _____ him today.
f The [football/soccer] match for Manchester United tomorrow is very important. They _____
g It's my mother's birthday next week. I _____ it.
h The floor is really dirty. You _____ it.
i Maria has an exam early tomorrow. She _____ early.
j Everything will be OK. You _____

☑ **Check the answers**

Now you

Write about two important things for you to do. Use _must_ and _mustn't_.

a _I must_ _____
b _I mustn't_ _____

35 | *Have to/had to* – for necessary actions
■ I have to leave
■ I had to leave

Meaning

1 Match the situations to the texts below.

a A man from Berlin talks about school.
b A teenage daughter at a party.
c A woman from London talks about school.
d Information about London Transport.

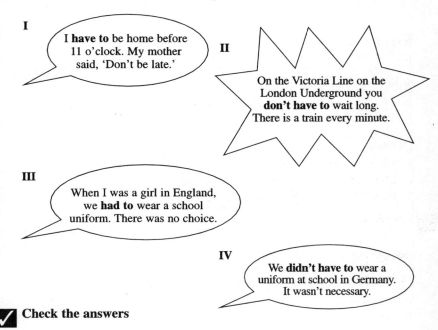

I

I **have to** be home before 11 o'clock. My mother said, 'Don't be late.'

II

On the Victoria Line on the London Underground you **don't have to** wait long. There is a train every minute.

III

When I was a girl in England, we **had to** wear a school uniform. There was no choice.

IV

We **didn't have to** wear a uniform at school in Germany. It wasn't necessary.

✓ **Check the answers**

2 Answer the questions about *have to* in the texts above.

a *Have to/don't have to* is for the future and general time. True or False?
b *Have to* is for something necessary. True or False?
c Is *have to* for when the speaker thinks something is necessary, or another person thinks something is necessary?
d *Don't have to* is for something not necessary. True or False?
e Is *had to/didn't have to* for the present or the past?

✓ **Check the answers**

Tip

Must is for when the **speaker** thinks something is necessary.
Have to is for when **another person** thinks something is necessary.
Mother to daughter, 'You *must* be home at 11:00.'
Daughter to her friend at the party, 'My mother wants me home at 11:00. I *have to* go.'
If you are not sure what to use, use *have to*.

Form

3 Complete the tables. The texts on page 153 will help. Use the words in the box.

| ~~he~~ | to | had | wait | didn't | don't | has | have |

Present

I We You They	**a** _____ to **b** _____ have **c** _____	go **d** _____
e *He* She It	**f** _____ to doesn't have to	

Past

I He She It We You They	**g** _____ to **h** _____ have to	go wait

Questions

Do	I/we/you/they	have to	go?
Does	he/she/it		
Did	I/we/you/they he/she/it		

 Check the answers

⚠ Common mistakes

4 **Correct the mistakes.**

a She have to leave now.
   She has to leave now.

b They have wait.

_____

c Have we to wait?

_____

d He not has to come.

_____

e We don't had to get up early.

_____

f You had to waited three hours.

_____

g Does she has to go now?

_____

 Check the answers

Practice

5 Complete the sentences.

a In some countries men have to   wear school uniforms.
b In England children have to   go now.
c Jean was a nurse and she had to   take a lot of exams.
d There's my train – I have to   work at night.
e In my final school year I had to   [do/complete] military service.

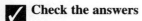 **Check the answers**

**6 Complete the sentences. Use *have to/has to/don't have to/doesn't have
to/had to/didn't have to* and a verb from the box.**

| g̶o̶   work   work   talk   answer   wear   get up   take |

a I ***don't have to go*** home – it's early, I can stay.
b The last bus had gone so I _____ a taxi.
c She's a doctor. She _____ really hard.
d The boss called. You _____ to him in his office.
e In the exam we _____ all of the questions. It was really
   difficult to finish.
f I had a day's [holiday/vacation] yesterday, I _____ early.
g In my job I _____ on Sundays. Sundays are always free.
h My eyes are terrible. I _____ glasses.

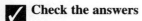 **Check the answers**

7 Put the words in the correct order to make questions.

a to uniform have do wear you a school ?
   Do you have to wear a school uniform?
b homework a lot of to you do did have at your old school ?
   _____
c your parents have school take to you did to ?
   _____
d most students jobs to have do have in your country ?
   _____
e the university system to have does accept all students ?
   _____

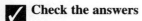 **Check the answers**

Now you

Write about two things that are necessary for you to do every day. Use *have to*.

a *I have to* _____

b *I* _____

Write about two things that are not necessary for you to do each day. Use *I don't have to*.

a *I don't have to* _____

b *I* _____

Write about two things that were necessary for you to do when you were a child. Use *I had to*.

a *I had to* _____

b *I* _____

Write about two things that were not necessary for you to do when you were a child. Use *I didn't have to*.

a *I didn't have to* _____

b *I* _____

➤ Unit 34 *must/mustn't* for obligation and prohibition

36 | Should/'d better – for advice
■ You should see a doctor
■ You'd better lie down

Meaning

1 Match the subjects to the texts.

a Advice about a job interview
b Advice about a visit to the Eiffel Tower in Paris
c Advice about the weather
d Advice about reading in English
e Advice about elephants in a safari park
f Advice about health

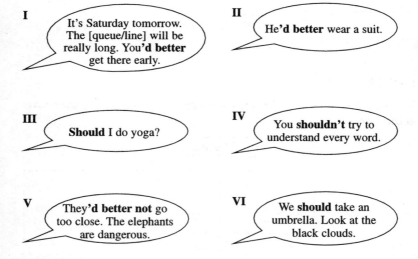

I It's Saturday tomorrow. The [queue/line] will be really long. You**'d better** get there early.

II He**'d better** wear a suit.

III **Should** I do yoga?

IV You **shouldn't** try to understand every word.

V They**'d better not** go too close. The elephants are dangerous.

VI We **should** take an umbrella. Look at the black clouds.

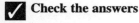 **Check the answers**

2 Answer the questions about the meaning of *should* **and** *'d better*.

'We should take an umbrella.'
a Is it a good idea to take an umbrella? Yes/No.
b Is this advice? Yes/No?

'You shouldn't try to understand every word.'
c Is it a good thing to try to understand every word? Yes/No
d Is this advice? Yes/No

'He'd better wear a suit.'
e Is it a good idea to wear a suit? Yes/No
f Is this advice? Yes/No

'They'd better not go too close.'
g Is it a good idea to go close? Yes/No
h Is this advice? Yes/No?

 Check the answers

Tip

should **or** *'d better* ?
'd better is for one action or one situation, but not for things in general.
Drivers ~~'d better~~ wear seat belts.
The situation is general so: Drivers should wear seat belts.
If you are not sure, use *should*.

Form

3 Complete the tables. The texts on page 158 will help. Use the words in the box.

~~eat~~	do	'd better	should

I He She It	**a** _____	(n't)	**c** *eat* fruit.
We You They	**b** _____	(not)	

Should	I he she it we you they	**d** _____ exercise ?

 Check the answers

Common mistakes

4 Correct the mistakes.

a You should to do exercise.
   You should do exercise.

b You shouldn't to smoke.
   _____

c She'd better to see a doctor.
   _____

d He not should eat red meat.
   _____

e Do we should leave early?
   _____

f You'd better seeing a doctor.
   _____

 Check the answers

Practice

5 Complete the advice for good health with *should* or *shouldn't*.

a	*You shouldn't*	smoke.
b	*You should*	eat fresh fruit.
c	_____	do exercise.
d	_____	drive everywhere.
e	_____	go to bed very late.
f	_____	walk a lot.

 Check the answers

6 Give advice to a friend. She has a job interview at a bank next week. She is always late. She only wears jeans. She doesn't smile. She doesn't ask questions. She smokes a lot. Put the words in the correct order.

a 'd late not you arrive better
   You'd better not arrive late.
b jeans not you better 'd wear
   _____
c better 'd smile you at the interviewer
   _____
d questions better you ask 'd some
   _____
e during the interview smoke you not better 'd
   _____

☑ **Check the answers**

7 You are going on [holiday/vacation]. Ask your friend for advice.

a You're not sure about buying a camera.
   Should I buy a camera?
b You're not sure about taking a sweater.
   Should I _____?
c You're not sure about going by bus.
   Should _____?
d You're not sure about taking [traveller's cheques/traveler's checks].
   _____?
e You're not sure about going at night.
   _____?

☑ **Check the answers**

Now you

Write sentences with *should*.

a *People should* _____
b *I should* _____

Write sentences with *shouldn't*.

c *People shouldn't* _____
d *I* _____

Write sentences with *'d better* and *'d better not*. Think about two
things for tomorrow.

e *I'd better* _____

f *I'd better not* _____

➤ Unit 34 *must/mustn't* for obligation and prohibition

37 Yes/no questions with be
■ Is it hard work?
■ Are the hours long?

Meaning

1 Jean thinks of a job. Tom asks questions to find out what the job is. Read the dialogue below and answer the question.

Is the job a teacher, a taxi driver or a nurse?

Tom	Jean
Is it hard work?	Yes, it is.
Are the hours long?	Yes, they are.
Is there a uniform?	Yes, there is.
Is the work inside or outside?	Inside.
Was there a lot of training?	Yes, there was.
Is the job always in one place?	Yes, it is.
Were you at work last night?	Yes, I was.

 Check the answer

Form

Making questions with be (am/is/are/was/were)

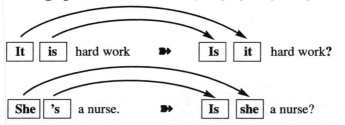

2 Make the questions.

a | The hours | | are | long. ➡ | | | long?

b | You | | are | a nurse. ➡ | | | a nurse?

c It was a good job.   ➡ | | | a good job?

d The money was good [in/at] your last job. ➡ _____ ___ _____
                                             good [in/at] your last job?

e You were working last night.   ➡ _____ working last night?

f He's a taxi driver.   ➡ _____ a taxi driver?

g They were unemployed.   ➡ _____?

 Check the answers

Tip

Questions with modal verbs (*can, could, will, would, may, might, must, should, ought*) are like questions with *be*.

| She | can | swim.   ➡ | **Can** | **she** | swim?

3 Complete the table. Use the words in the box.

| ~~am~~ they was I are |

Questions with *be*

a *Am* Was	**d** ___	
Is **b** ___	he she it	in the photo ?
c ___ Were	we you **e** ___	

 Check the answers

⚠ Common mistakes

4 Correct the mistakes. Put ☑ for a correct sentence and ☒ for an incorrect sentence.

a Was she a taxi driver?   ☑   e Were they all doctors? ☐
b She was a taxi driver?   ☒   f Was they all doctors? ☐
c Were I in the right job?   ☐   g She teacher?   ☐
d Was I in the right job?   ☐   h Is she a teacher?   ☐

✓ Check the answers

Practice

5 Make questions. Use the words in the circle. Use the words more than once if necessary.

last night   now
was
were   am   Jon
Jean and David
we   I   OK
are   is
?

a *Was I OK last night?*
b _____?
c _____?
d _____?
e _____?
f _____?
g _____?
h _____?

✓ Check the answers

6 First make questions. Then read the answers to find the job.

a money/good   *Is the money good?*   No, it isn't.
b hours/long   _____?   Yes, they are.
c work/hard   _____?   Yes, it is.

d there/uniform   _____?   No, there isn't.
e work/at home   _____?   Yes, it is.
f Is it a housewife or an office cleaner?

✓ **Check the answers**

Now you

You meet someone at a party. Ask three questions.

a *Are you*_____?
b _____?
c _____?

➤ Unit 38 *Yes/no questions* with *do*

38 | *Yes/no questions* with *do*
■ Do you wear a uniform?
■ Does the job have training?

Meaning

1 Jean thinks of a job. Tom asks questions to find out what the job is. Read the dialogue below and answer the question.

Is the job an architect, a plumber or a builder?

Tom	Jean
Do you wear a uniform?	No, I don't.
Do you work with buildings?	Yes, I do.
Does the job have a lot of training?	Yes, it does.
Do you work with water?	No, I don't.
Do you work with electricity?	No, I don't.
Did you want the job when you were small?	No, I didn't.
Did you go to [university/college]?	Yes, I did.
Do you design houses?	Yes, I do.

✓ Check the answer

Form

Making questions with *do*

Present Simple

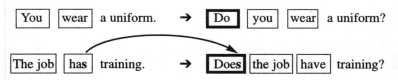

| You | wear | a uniform. | → | **Do** | you | wear | a uniform? |

| The job | has | training. | → | **Does** | the job | have | training? |

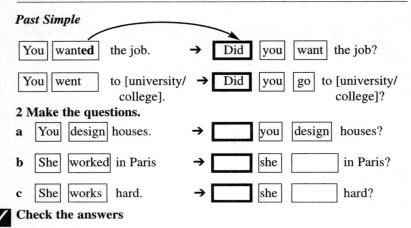

Past Simple

| You | wanted | the job. | → | Did | you | want | the job? |

| You | went | to [university/ | → | Did | you | go | to [university/ |
| | | college]. | | | | | college]? |

2 Make the questions.

a | You | design | houses. | → | _____ | you | design | houses?

b | She | worked | in Paris | → | _____ | she | _____ | in Paris?

c | She | works | hard. | → | _____ | she | _____ | hard?

☑ **Check the answers**

Tip

Present Simple
Only one –*s* with the third person singular.
She like*s* her job. → Doe*s* she like her job?

3 Complete the tables. Use the words in the box.

| I̶ | it | does | work | do |

Questions with *do*

Present Simple		
a ____	c / we you they	work ?
b ____	he she d ____	

Past Simple		
Did	I he she it we you they	e ____?

✓ Check the answers

⚠ Common mistakes

4 Correct the mistakes. Put ☑ for a correct sentence and ☒ for an incorrect sentence.

a Does she like her job? ☑
b Does she likes her job? ☒
c You like your job? ☐
d Do you like your job? ☐

e Did they liked their jobs? ☐
f Did they like their jobs? ☐
g Do he likes his job? ☐
h Does he like his job? ☐

Check the answers

✓ Practice

5 Make questions. Use the words in the circle. Use the words again if necessary.

in Canada
does   do   did
live
Jean and David
she   last year
Jon
?

a *Do Jean and David live in Canada?*
b _____?

c _____?
d _____?
e _____?
f _____?

✓ **Check the answers**

6 First make questions. Then read the answers and find the job.

a you/earn/good money   *Do you earn good money?* Yes, I do.
b you/work/long hours   _____? No, I don't.
c you/study/for the job   _____? Yes, I did.
d the job/need/special equipment _____? Yes, it does.
e the job/make you happy   _____? Yes, it does.
f Is it a photographer or a policeman?

✓ **Check the answers**

Now you

You meet someone at a party. Ask four questions. Use *do/does/did*.

a *Do you*_____?
b *Do* _____?
c *Did* _____?
d _____?

➤ Unit 37 *Yes/no questions* with *be*

Wh- questions
■ Where do you work?
■ What did you see?

Meaning

1 What is the dialogue about?

How many do you have?	About 20,000.
Where do you get them?	[Shops, specialist shops/Stores, speciality stores]. And from my mother. She works at an English school in Oxford. They get letters from a lot of different countries.
What do you do with them?	Look at them, show my friends!
Why do you collect them?	For fun and because they are valuable.
Which is the best one?	This one from Honduras.
When did you get it?	About 5 years ago.

✓ **Check the answer**

2 Match a question word with an answer.

a What?   5 years ago
b Who?   My mother
c Where?   Because they're valuable
d Why?   By [post/mail]
e How?   Stamps
f When?   It's Paul's
g Whose?   The one from Honduras
h Which?   From [shops/stores]

✓ **Check the answers**

Form

3 Complete the tables. Use the words in the box.

~~you~~	where	was	play	whose	do

| When
a ____
Who
How
What
Why
Which
Whose | **b** ____
   did | **c** *you* | **d** ____ ?
   see |
| When
Where
Who
How
What
Why
Which
e ____ | is
f ____ | it
he ? | |

✓ Check the answers

⚠Common mistakes

4 Put ☑ for a correct sentence and ☒ for an incorrect sentence.

a Where does live John? ☑
b Where does John live? ☒
c What music you like ? ☐
d What music do you like? ☐
e What does 'fluent' mean? ☐
f What means 'fluent'? ☐
g Where did she went? ☐
h Where did she go? ☐
i What you said? ☐
j What did you say? ☐

✓ Check the answers

Tip

| What do you do? = What is your job?

Practice

5 Make questions with *when* and *where*. Use the words in the circle. Use the words more than once if necessary.

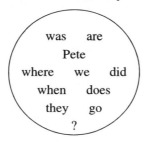

was   are
Pete
where   we   did
when   does
they   go
?

a   *Where are they?*

b _____?

c _____?

d _____?

e _____?

f _____?

 Check the answers

6 Write *wh-* questions to find the information to fill the spaces.

Jerry lives in __(a)__. She has a house and four dogs and a cat.
She likes animals because __(b)__. Every day she gets up at __(c)__ and
takes the dogs for a walk. She moved into the house in 19 __(d)__.
She goes to work by __(e)__. She meets __(f)__ at the station.
Last year she changed her job because __(g)__.

a   *Where does Jerry live?*

b   *Why does* _____?

c   *What* _____?

d   *Wh* _____?

e   _____?

f   _____?

g   _____?

 Check the answers

Now you

You meet someone at a party. Ask three questions.

a *Where* _____?
b *What* _____?
c *Wh* _____?

➤ Unit 37 *Yes/no questions* with *be*
➤ Unit 38 *Yes/no questions* with *do*
➤ Unit 40 *Wh- questions* for subject and object

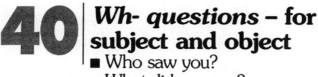

40 | Wh- questions – for subject and object
■ Who saw you?
■ What did you see?

Meaning

1 Match the pictures and the news stories below.

a   b

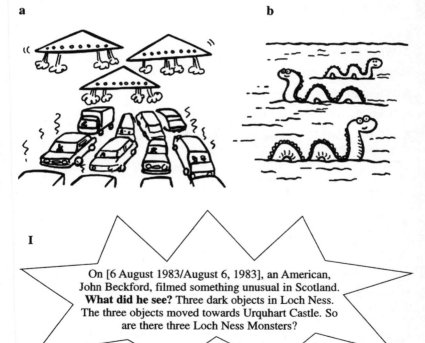

I

On [6 August 1983/August 6, 1983], an American,
John Beckford, filmed something unusual in Scotland.
What did he see? Three dark objects in Loch Ness.
The three objects moved towards Urquhart Castle. So
are there three Loch Ness Monsters?

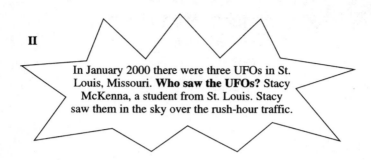

II

In January 2000 there were three UFOs in St. Louis, Missouri. **Who saw the UFOs?** Stacy McKenna, a student from St. Louis. Stacy saw them in the sky over the rush-hour traffic.

 Check the answers

2 What did he see?

Is 'what' the subject or the object of the verb 'see'?

3 Who saw the UFOs?

Is 'who' the subject or the object of the verb 'saw'?

4 Put the words *object* or *subject* into the boxes.

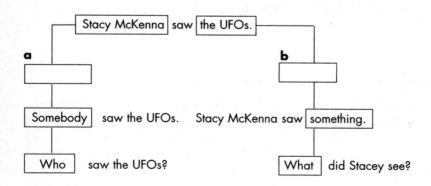

Stacy McKenna | saw | the UFOs.

a   **b**

Somebody | saw the UFOs.   Stacy McKenna saw | something.

Who | saw the UFOs?   What | did Stacey see?

Check the answers

Form

5 Complete the tables with the words in the box.

~~who~~	did	broke

a *Who* What	**b** _____ the window?

[Who/whom] What	do **c** _____	you	like? see?

 Check the answers

Tip

Learn this rhyme:

What did you say?
I said something funny.
What did you pay?
I paid the money.
Who said something funny?
It was my mother.
Who paid the money?
It was my brother.

⚠Common mistakes

6 Put ☑ for a correct sentence and ☒ for an incorrect sentence.

a Who saw a monster? ☑
b Who did see a monster? ☒
c What you saw? ☐
d What did you see? ☐
e [Who/whom] you did see? ☐
f [Who/whom] did you see? ☐
g What did you see? ☐
h What did you saw? ☐
i What means this word? ☐
j What does this word mean? ☐

 Check the answers

Practice

7 Make questions. Use the words in the circle. Use the words more than once if necessary.

the man
shoot   did
[who/whom]
shot   what   likes
does   like   ?

a *What does the man like?*
b _____?
c _____?
d _____?
e _____?

✓ **Check the answers**

8 Ask questions.

a   b

Who *shot George*?   [Who/whom] _____?

c

d

[Who/whom] *does Mary love*?   Who _____?

 Check the answers

9 Make questions with *who* or *what*.

a Somebody lives here.
Who *lives here*?

b Somebody said something.
Who _____?

c Something happened.
What _____?

d Peter said something.
What did _____?

e Jean saw something.
What _____?

f Andrew did something.
_____?

g Somebody knows the answer.
_____?

 Check the answers

Now you

Write two questions to ask a friend.

a *What did* _____?

b *Who* _____?

41 Echo questions
- Have you?
- Are you?
- Don't you?

Meaning

1 Match the pictures with the conversations below and overleaf.

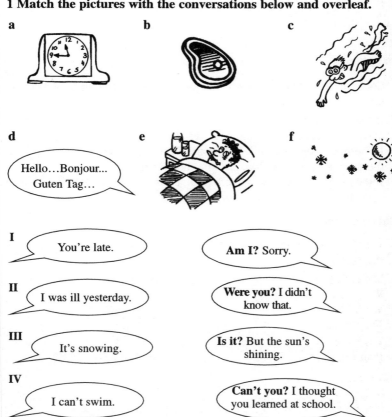

a (clock)

b (palette)

c (swimmer)

d Hello...Bonjour... Guten Tag...

e (person ill in bed)

f (snowflakes and sun)

I You're late. — **Am I?** Sorry.

II I was ill yesterday. — **Were you?** I didn't know that.

III It's snowing. — **Is it?** But the sun's shining.

IV I can't swim. — **Can't you?** I thought you learned at school.

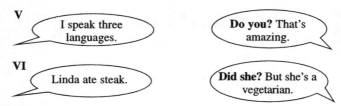

V
I speak three languages.

Do you? That's amazing.

VI
Linda ate steak.

Did she? But she's a vegetarian.

✓ **Check the answers**

2 The questions in bold are *echo questions*. Answer the questions about echo questions.

a Echo questions show interest. Yes/No?
b Echo questions sometimes show surprise. Yes/No?

✓ **Check the answers**

Form

3 Look at the echo questions in the dialogues above. Answer the questions about their form.

a If the main verb is *be* (am/is/are/was/were), which verb is in the echo question? *Be*, *do*, *did* or a modal verb?
b If the main verb is a full verb in the *Present Simple*, which verb is in the echo question? *Be*, *do*, *did* or a modal verb?
c If the main verb is a modal verb (*can, must, may,* etc.), which verb is in the echo question? *Be*, *do*, *did* or a modal verb?

✓ **Check the answers**

4 Match the echo questions with the sentences.

a I'm late.   Isn't she?
b She isn't late.   Am I?
c We're late.   Are you?
d You're late.   Are they?
e They're late.   Can she?
f They were late.   Are you?
g Jean can swim.   Were they?

5 Put the words in the correct box.

| ~~I don't smoke.~~ | We smoke. | Did they? | Doesn't she? |

a | *I don't smoke.* | Don't you?

b She doesn't smoke.   [   ]

c [   ]   Do you?

d They smoked before.   [   ]

✔ **Check the answers**

⚠ Common mistakes

6 Put ☑ for correct sentences and ☒ for incorrect sentences.

a **A** I do yoga. **B** Do you? ☑   **e** **A** I'm French. **B** Am I? ☐
b **A** I do yoga. **B** Don't you? ☒   **f** **A** I'm French. **B** Are you? ☐
c **A** I like football. **B** Is it? ☐   **g** **A** I played football. **B** Did you? ☐
d **A** I like football. **B** Do you? ☐   **h** **A** I played football. **B** Didn't you? ☐

✔ **Check the answers**

Tip

To show interest, the *music* (your voice) goes up.

The music goes up ↑ in an echo question.

I'm not hungry. Aren't you?

Practice

7 Show interest. Use an echo question.

a Hello, I'm from Hong Kong.   *Are you*?
b Yes, I live in Bangkok now.   *Do* _____?
c I work at a bank here.   _____?
d I'm married.   _____?

e Yes, my wife doesn't like big cities.   _____?
f No, she lived in the country before we married. _____?
g I don't like the country.   _____?
h My children go to school here.   _____?
i They can speak English and Thai.   _____?

 Check the answers

➤ Unit 37 *Yes/no questions* with *be*
➤ Unit 38 *Yes/no questions* with *do*
➤ Unit 39 *Wh- questions*
➤ Unit 40 *Wh- questions* for subject and object

42 | *Embedded questions*
■ Can you tell me where the station is?
■ Do you know what the time is?

Meaning

1 Match the best picture to the dialogue below.

a

b

c

d

A Excuse me, **can you tell me what time the bus comes?**
B The bus?
A Yes, *what time does the bus come?*
B Err, **I don't know what time the bus comes**.
A What about the train? **Can you tell me what time the train leaves?**
B The train?
A Yes, *what time does the train leave?*
B Err, **I don't know what time the train leaves**.
Wait a minute…
A Yes.
B It's Sunday. There are no buses or trains.

 Check the answer

2 Look at the questions in the dialogue above.

The questions in *italics* are direct questions. The questions in **bold** are embedded questions. Which is more polite?

3 After 'I don't know…' is there a direct question or an embedded question?

 Check the answers

Form

Questions with *be (am/are/is/was/were)*

When [is] [the meeting]? → Can you tell me when [the meeting] [is]?

4 Complete the boxes.

a Who [is] [she]?   → Can you tell me who [   ] [   ]?

b Where is the station? → Can you tell me _____?

Questions with *do/does/did*

What time [does the train leave]? → *Can you tell me* what time [the train leaves]?

5 Complete the boxes.

a What [does she want]? → *Can you tell me* what _____?

b Why [did she go]?   → *Can you tell me* why _____ _____?

c What [did he want]?   → *Can you tell me* what _____ _____?

d Where [did they stay]? → *Can you tell me* where _____ _____?

 Check the answers

Common mistakes

6 Put ☑ for correct sentences and ☒ for incorrect sentences.

a Can you tell me where she is? ☑   **d** Can you tell me what it is?   ☐
b Can you tell me where is she? ☒   **e** Do you know where she lives? ☐
c Can you tell me what is it?   ☐   **f** Do you know where lives she? ☐

g I know why he called. ☐
h I know why did he call. ☐

i I can't remember when does
   he leave. ☐
j I can't remember when he
   leaves. ☐

✓ **Check the answers**

Tip

a Do you know what she reads? ✓
~~Do you know what does she read?~~

b Yes/No questions: use *if* or *whether.*
Is John there?
→ Do you know **if** John is there?
Does Mary smoke?
→ I don't know **whether** Mary smokes.

Practice

7 Make the questions polite! You are talking to a stranger in the street.

a Where is the police station?
Can you tell me *where the police station is, please*?
b Where is the nearest bank?
Can you tell me _____?
c What time does the next bus come?
Can you tell _____?
d Where is the museum?
Can you _____?
e What is the time?
Can _____?
f How far is the station?
_____?

✓ **Check the answers**

8 Put the words in the correct order to make sentences.

a where I don't know Susan lives
I don't know where Susan lives.

b know Susan where lives you do ?
   Do you _____

c I can't remember Susan is where
   I can't _____

d know her job what I is
   _____

e know they went I don't where
   _____

Now you

Think of three questions to ask a stranger at a train station or an airport. Use *Can you tell me...*? or *Do you know...*?

a *Do you know* _____? ?

b _____? ?

c _____? ?

➤ Unit 37 *Yes/no questions* with *be*
➤ Unit 38 *Yes/no questions* with *do*
➤ Unit 39 *Wh- questions*
➤ Unit 40 *Wh- questions* for subject and object
➤ Unit 41 *Echo questions*

43 | Verbs + gerund, verbs + infinitive
■ It stopped raining
■ I want to leave now

Meaning

1 Match the pictures to the plans below.

a

b

c

d

e

f

I

> There is no work here. **I'd like** to go to the U.S.A. next year and find a job there.

II

> **I like** cooking. I cook a lot. And **I love** eating Indian food. One day **I hope** to have a vegetarian Indian restaurant.

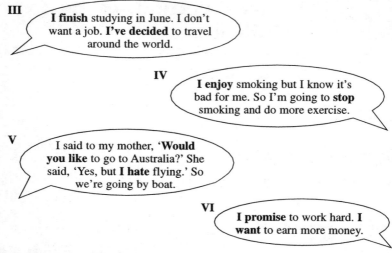

III

I **finish** studying in June. I don't want a job. **I've decided** to travel around the world.

IV

I **enjoy** smoking but I know it's bad for me. So I'm going to **stop** smoking and do more exercise.

V

I said to my mother, '**Would you like** to go to Australia?' She said, 'Yes, but **I hate** flying.' So we're going by boat.

VI

I **promise** to work hard. I **want** to earn more money.

✓ **Check the answers**

2 Answer the questions about *like* in the texts above.

a 'I like cooking.' Is this about one meal or cooking in general?

b 'I'd like to go to the U.S.A...' Is this about one visit to the U.S.A. or visits to the U.S.A. in general?

✓ **Check the answers**

Form

3 Some verbs are followed by the *infinitive* (I promise *to work*). Some verbs are followed by the gerund (I hate *flying*).

Look at the speech bubbles on pages 189 and 190 and put the verbs in the box in the correct list.

'd like	like	love	hope	finish	decide	enjoy	stop
		hate	promise	want			

Verbs + infinitive	Verbs + gerund
'd like	_____
_____	_____
_____	_____
_____	_____
_____	_____

✓ **Check the answers**

⚠ Common mistakes

4 Put ☑ for correct sentences and ☒ for incorrect sentences.

a It stopped raining. ☑
b It stopped to rain. ☒
c They want leave. ☐
d They want to leave. ☐
e Do you like to leave now? ☐
f Would you like to leave now? ☐

g I'd like to go out tonight. ☐
h I'd like going out tonight. ☐
i When do you finish to work?☐
j When do you finish working?☐
k I hope see you next week. ☐
l I hope to see you next week. ☐

✓ **Check the answers**

Tip

Main verb + infinitive
Often the main verb happens first.
I want *to go*. 'want' happens before 'go'.

past	now	future
	I want	to go

Main verb + gerund
Often the main verb happens second.
It stopped *raining*. 'stopped' happened after 'raining'.

past	now	future
raining stopped		

Practice

5 Choose the correct form of the verbs in the letter.

> *Dear John,*
>
> *This is a difficult letter to write. I've decided (a) to stay/~~staying~~
> here in Italy for another year. I know I promised (b) to come/coming
> home next month but I like (c) to live/living here. I'd like (d) to
> find/finding a job here. I met someone here last month and I like
> him a lot. We're hoping (e) to find/finding a house together. I still
> want (f) to write/writing to you. I will always love you and I will
> never stop (g) to think/thinking about you. If you want (h) to
> go/going out with other girls, of course I understand. Please write
> to me. When I finish (i) to write/writing this letter, I'm going to go
> to bed and cry.*
>
> *All my love,*
>
> *Sally*

 Check the answers

6 Choose the correct form of the verb.

a Bill *Would you like to go / ~~Do you like going~~* to the [cinema/movies]?
   Ben No, not tonight. I've got homework.
b Bill *Would you like to play / Do you like playing* tennis?
   Ben I'd like to but I can't today.
c Bill *Would you like to go/ Do you like going* out to eat?
   Ben Yes, I do. Arabic food is my [favourite/favorite].
d Bill *Would you like to /Do you like to* watch TV?
   Ben What's on at the moment?
e Bill *Would you like to go to a rock concert?/ Do you like going to rock
       concerts?*
f Ben Yes, I often go with friends.

 Check the answers

7 *Would you like to...* and *Do you like + -ing*

Put the verb in brackets ( ) in the correct form: *to...* **or** *-ing.*

a I'd like *to meet* (meet) you.
b Do you like _____ (read)?
c What would you like _____ (do) tonight?
d My sister is a teacher but she doesn't like _____ (teach).
e Jean would like _____ (find) a bigger house.

✓ **Check the answers**

Now you

Write sentences about you.

a *I like* _____
b *I hate* _____
c *I want to* _____
d *I'd like to* _____
e *I'm going to stop* _____
f *I hope to* _____

➤ Unit 19 *going to* for future plans

44 Articles *a/an/the/* – indefinite, definite and no article

■ a thief
■ an egg
■ the thief
■ in England

Meaning

1 Find the answer to the question in the story below. The story is about a thief in a supermarket.

Did the thief have more money when he left the supermarket? Yes/No.

A thief went into **a** supermarket in Russell Street in Southampton, **a** town in England. It was **an** expensive [shop/store] and **the** biggest supermarket in **the** town. **The** thief put cans in **a** basket. He took **the** basket to **a** [checkout/checkout line] and gave **the** cashier £100. When she opened her register, there was only one £50 [note/bill] in it. He was shocked. He took **the** £50 [note/bill] and ran. **The** thief was **a** cashier in another supermarket.

 Check the answer

2 Match the articles (*a*, *the*) from the story with the uses. It is possible to match the examples with more than one use.

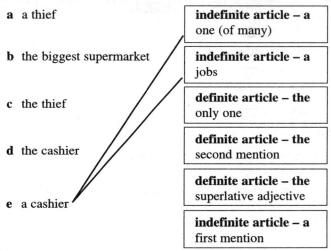

a a thief

indefinite article – a
one (of many)

b the biggest supermarket

indefinite article – a
jobs

c the thief

definite article – the
only one

d the cashier

definite article – the
second mention

definite article – the
superlative adjective

e a cashier

indefinite article – a
first mention

✓ **Check the answers**

3 Match the examples of zero article (no article) with the uses.

a in Russell Street

zero article
towns

b in Southampton

zero article
countries

c in England

zero article
streets and roads

✓ **Check the answers**

4 Match some more examples of zero article with the uses.

a What do you want for breakfast? ⎤
   Dinner is ready!   ⎦

zero article
general meaning

b I'm going to work, you're going to
   school, Jean's in church, Dad's in
   prison, Pete's in bed, and the cat's
   at home!

zero article
meals

c I like rock music and classical music. ⎤
   All you need is love.   ⎥
   I hate examinations.   ⎬
   Courage is important.   ⎥
   Flowers are beautiful.   ⎦

zero article
common places with
prepositions

d My [favourite/favorite] sports are tennis,
   swimming and skiing.

zero article
sports and games

e English is easy, physics and history
   are difficult.

zero article
academic subjects

✓ **Check the answers**

5 Match the examples of the definite article with the uses.

a The sky is blue. Is the moon blue? ⎤
   The president of the U.S.A.   ⎦

definite article
entertainments

b My sister is in the army.   ⎤
   I'll phone the police.   ⎥
   First I'll go to the bank   ⎬
   and then the dentist.   ⎦

definite article
institutions

c What's on the radio?   ⎤
   Turn off the TV, let's go to the [cinema/ ⎬
   movies]or the opera.   ⎦

definite article
uniqueness/only one

d The Atlantic, the Mediterranean and
   the Nile – that's a lot of water!

definite article
rivers and oceans

e I've been to the Netherlands, the
   Philippines, and the Andes.

definite article
plural countries,
plural mountains

✓ **Check the answers**

Form

A or *an*?

a thief in a supermarket	an expensive supermarket
a town	an orange
a basket	an apple
a cashier	an ice cube
a hotel	an umbrella
a university (pronounced 'yuniversity')	an hour (pronounced 'our')
a European (pronounced 'yuropean')	an M.A. (pronounced 'emmay')
a use (pronounced 'yuse')	

6 Complete the rule with *a* or *an*.

_____ before vowel sounds.

_____ before consonant sounds.

✓ Check the answers

⚠ Common mistakes

7 Put ☑ for correct sentences and ☒ for incorrect sentences.

a I'm living in the Prague.

b I'm living in Prague.

c I have small house.

d I have a small house.

e My house is in the country.

f My house is in city country.

g I've got a new job.

h I've got new job.

i I'm cashier in a supermarket. ☐

j I'm a cashier in a supermarket. ☐

k The supermarket sells only organic food. ☐

l The supermarket sells only the organic food. ☐

m I play the football in my free time. ☐

n I play football in my free time. ☐

☑ **j**   ☒ **k**

☐ **a**   ☐ **b**   ☐ **c**   ☐ **d**   ☐ **e**   ☐ **f**   ☐ **g**   ☐ **h**

✓ Check the answers

Tip

Small Difference – *big difference*

Katie's at school.	Katie's at **the** school.
She's a student.	*She's a visitor.*
Katie's in prison.	Katie's in **the** prison.
She's a criminal.	*She's a visitor.*
Katie's at [university/college].	Katie's at **the** [university/college].
She's a student.	*She's a visitor.*

Practice

8 Complete the jobs with *a* or *an*.

a   *a*   dentist
b   ____   politician
c   ____   electrician
d   ____   manager
e   ____   housewife
f   ____   university professor
g   ____   European member of parliament
h   ____   Indian-restaurant owner

✓ **Check the answers**

9 Zero article: make true sentences with columns A, B and C.

A	B	C
Cats	can't	oil and [petrol/gas].
Wine	like	from grapes.
Elephants	is	to school.
Children	need	jump.
Cars	go	full of vitamins.
Fruit	comes	fish.

a *Cats like fish.*
b *Wine comes* _____
c *Elephants* _____
d *Children* _____
e *Cars* _____
f _____

✓ **Check the answers**

10 Complete with *a*, *an*, *the*, or nothing (zero article).

Brad lives in (**a**) ***the*** United States. He's got (**b**) ____ big house in (**c**)____ California. (**d**) ____ house is in (**e**)____ Malibu on (**f**)____ Pacific Ocean. Malibu is (**g**) ____ expensive place. Brad has got (**h**) ____ good job. He's (**i**)____ lawyer.

✓ **Check the answers**

11 Circle ◯ the correct article: *a/an/the/–* (zero).

a When you come to *a/an/the/* ⊖ bed, please turn off the lights.
b We went to a restaurant last night. What was the name of *a/an/the/* – restaurant?
c I arrive at *a/an/the/–* school at 8.30.
d At *a/an/the/–* school I studied *a/an/the/–* French.
e Ankara is the capital of *a/an/the/–* Turkey.
f She was at *a/an/the/–* home all day today.
g Heathrow is *a/an/the/–* busiest airport in *a/an/the/–* Europe.
h I love *a/an/the/–* cheese.
i Where are *a/an/the/–* children? In the park.
j *a/an/the/–* children are hard work for parents.

✓ **Check the answers**

Now you

Write sentences about you. Think about articles.

a Your job. *I'm* _____
b [Favourite/Favorite] school subject. *I like* _____
c [Favourite/Favorite] sport. *I like* _____
d Your country. *I live in* _____
e Entertainment. *I like* _____
f Regular meal. *I eat* _____ *at* _____

45 | Singular and plural nouns
■ car/cars
■ child/children

Meaning

1 Match the titles to the texts below.

a Buildings
b Population
c [Transport/Transportation]

Information about Britain in the 1990s

I
There were about 60 million people in Britain in the 1990s.
23,828,000 women
22,872,000 men
11,700,000 children (5,967,000 girls and 5,733,000 boys)

II
There were 28,150 churches, 23,000,000 houses and 160,400 factories.

III
There were 71,000 buses, 2,000,000 [lorries/trucks] and 20,700,000 cars.

 Check the answers

Form

2 Find the plural of the nouns in the texts above.

Singular	Plural
a person	*people*
b woman	_____
c man	_____
d child	_____
e church	_____
f house	_____
g factory	_____
h bus	_____
i [lorry /truck]	_____
j car	_____

 Check the answers

Spelling

3 Complete the spelling rules for plural nouns.

a car	⇨ cars			
After most nouns add **-s**		week	⇨	_**weeks**_
b story	⇨ stor**ies**			
After consonant + -y, add -_ _ _		factory	⇨	_____
c holiday	⇨ holidays			
After vowel + -y, add -_		boy	⇨	_____
d dish	⇨ dish**es**			
After -sh, add -_ _		wish	⇨	_____
e church	⇨ church**es**			
After -ch, add -_ _		watch	⇨	_____
f bus	⇨ bus**es**			
After -s, add -_ _		kiss	⇨	_____

 Check the answers

4 Here are some more spelling rules for plural nouns. Can you complete them?

a box	⇨ box**es**		
After -x, add -_ _		fox	⇨ _____

b shelf   ⇨   shel**ves**
   wife   ⇨   wi**ves**

After -f, ⎫
After -fe, ⎬ add -_ _ _   loaf   ⇨ _____

c radio   ⇨   radio**s**

After vowel + -o, add -_   video   ⇨ _____

d tomato   ⇨   tomato**es**

After consonant + -o, add -_ _   potato   ⇨ _____

e Two irregular nouns with consonant + -o.
   photo   ⇨   photo**s**
   piano   ⇨   piano**s**

✓ **Check the answers**

5 Some nouns are irregular. Complete the irregular plurals from the jumbled letters.

a	man	⇨ ***men***	(nme)
b	woman	⇨ _____	(nemwo)
c	child	⇨ _____	(renchild)
d	person	⇨ _____	(lepeop)
e	tooth	⇨ _____	(eetth)
f	foot	⇨ _____	(eeft)
g	sheep	⇨ _____	(eeshp)
h	fish	⇨ _____	(shfi)
i	mouse	⇨ _____	(icem)

✓ **Check the answers**

⚠ Common mistakes

6 Choose the correct spelling for each noun.

a ~~buss~~/buses
b childs/children
c sandwiches/sandwichs
d teachers/teacheres
e churchs/churches
f factorys/factories
g boys/boies
h watchs/watches

i noses/nosies
j cameraes/cameras
k leafs/leaves
l mice/mices
m womens/women

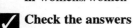 **Check the answers**

Practice

7 Complete the sentences. Use the words in the box. Put the words in the plural.

~~potato~~	day	child	zoo	dish	tooth	key	video
		glass	match	photo			

a I like a lot of *potatoes* with my dinner.
b Can you wash the _____ ?
c There are seven _____ in a week.
d Where are my _____ ? I want to make a fire.
e There are no _____ in my country. Where can I see elephants and lions?
f Can I see the _____ you took on [holiday/vacation]?
g I'd like to watch one of your _____ .
h My friend has a big family. She's had seven _____ .
i We need the wine _____ for dinner.
j Brush your _____ before you go to bed!
k Where are my car _____ ?

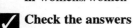 **Check the answers**

Tip

The *person* in the car. ⇨ The *people* in the car.
Person can be plural but it is very formal.

For example, in signs:
This [lift/elevator] can carry 8 *persons*.
This taxi can carry 6 *persons*.

Now you

Write sentences about you. Use the plural of these words:

| foot | child | video | potato | tomato | city |

a *I have big/small/medium* _____
b *I like* _____
c *I don't like* _____
d *I like* _____
e *I* _____
f _____

46 | Subject and object pronouns
■ It's for me
■ I like him

Meaning

1 Match the situations to the texts below.

a A thank-you present
b A birthday telephone call
c Shopping for clothes
d Twins' birthday cards

e An office phone call
f [Holiday/Vacation] photographs
g Romantic problems
h Lost children

I   **A** Hello, *John* speaking.
    B Happy Birthday!
    A Oh, thank you. Wait a minute, I think I've got some letters here. Yes, they are all for **me**!

II *Peter*, you were so nice to me. The flowers are for **you**.

III **A** Phone call for *Mr. Evans*.
    B He doesn't work here now. Are you sure the call's for **him**?

IV **A** I like *Mary* a lot. She's wonderful.
    B But do you love **her**?
    A I'm not sure.

V   I like *the black dress*. And it's not expensive. I'm going to buy **it**.

VI Here are *my photos*. They're all of Greece. Would you like to look at **them**?

VII Where are *the children*? Oh, it's OK. They're here under the table! I thought we'd lost **them**.

VIII **A** Happy Birthday, *Sally and Joan*.
     Sally and Joan Thank you. Look, we've got some letters. Yes, they're all for **us**!

✓ **Check the answers**

Look at the texts on page 205. The nouns are *in italics,* the subject pronouns are <u>underlined</u> and the object pronouns are **in bold**.

A Phone call for *Mr. Evans.* B <u>He</u> doesn't work here now. Are you sure the call's for **him**?

Form

2 **Complete the table. Use the texts on page 205 to help you.**

Noun	Subject pronoun	Object pronoun
John	I	**a** *me*
Peter	you	**b** _____
Mr. Evans	he	**c** _____
Mary	**d** _____	her
e _____	it	it
f _____	they	**g** _____
the children	**h** _____	**i** _____
Sally and Joan	we	**j** _____

✔ **Check the answers**

Tip

For things, we use *it* (singular) and *them* (plural).
There's *my new car.* Do you like **it**?
Here are *my new shoes.* Do you like **them**?

⚠ Common mistakes

3 **Put ☑ for correct sentences and ☒ for incorrect sentences.**

a Paul thinks Paula is horrible. He doesn't like her. ☑
b Paul thinks Paula is horrible. He doesn't like she. ☒
c Paula likes the boys in the car. She thinks them are handsome. ☐
d Paula likes the boys in the car. She thinks they are handsome. ☐

e Paula likes Pete but she doesn't want to marry him.☐
f Paula likes Peter but she doesn't want to marry he. ☐
g I like you but do you like I? ☐
h I like you but do you like me? ☐
i The bottles are in the sun. Put them in the fridge. ☐
j The bottles are in the sun. Put it in the fridge. ☐

✓ **Check the answers**

Practice

4 Complete the sentences with *me/us/you/him/her/them/it.*

a Who is that man? Why are you looking at ***him***?
b We are going to the [cinema/movies]. Do you want to come with ____?
c Do you know John? Yes, I work with ____
d That cheese is bad. Don't eat ____
e Where are my car keys? I can't find ____
f I don't know Jean and Mary. Do you know ____?
g I want your help. Please listen to ____
h Is this a photo of Jane? I don't really know ____
i Where's the bank? ____ is opposite the station.
j I hear you're going to the [theatre/theater]. Can I come with ____?

✓ **Check the answers**

5 Replace the ~~deleted~~ words with a subject or object pronoun.

James loves Barbara but ~~Barbara~~ (**a**) *she* doesn't love ~~James~~ (**b**) _____.
I wrote to my new girlfriend but ~~my new girlfriend~~ (**c**) _____ didn't send a reply.
My friends came to stay with me but I didn't want ~~my friends~~ (**d**) _____ to stay.
My wife and I have three children but ~~the three children~~ (**e**) _____ never visit ~~my wife and me~~ (**f**) _____.

✓ **Check the answers**

47 | Countable and uncountable nouns – *some/any/much/many/a lot of* – nouns and quantifiers

■ I've got some food
■ I haven't got any pasta
■ There's a lot of food
■ Have we got much food?
■ There aren't many oranges

Meaning

1 Read the dialogue below. Henry and Henrietta are talking about the food they have in the kitchen. Henrietta is in the kitchen, Henry is in the sitting room. Look at the picture. Is this the food they have? Yes/No

Henry	What's for dinner?
Henrietta	Well, there are **a lot of** *tomatoes* and there's **a lot of** *pasta*. And, yes, there's **some** *cheese* and **a lot of** *onions*. And we've got **some** *salt* and *pepper*.
Henry	OK, let's have *spaghetti*. Have we got **any** *mushrooms*?

Henrietta	No, there aren't **any** *mushrooms*, I'm afraid. But we can have *salad*. We've got **some** *lettuce*.
Henry	What about drinks? Have we got **much** *wine*? Would you like **some** *wine*?
Henrietta	No, we haven't got **much** *wine* – half a glass. But there are **some** *oranges*...
Henry	**How many** *oranges*?
Henrietta	Well, we haven't got **many** oranges – only three.
Henry	OK, not **much** *orange juice*, then. And not **much** *wine*.
Henrietta	But a lot of *pasta*!

 Check the answer

Some nouns can be *countable* (two lettuces) and *uncountable* (Do you want some lettuce?). Sometimes the countable noun means kinds or types (The wines they make in France.).

Countable   **Uncountable**

lettuces   lettuce

cheeses   cheese

wines   wine

2 Look at the nouns *in italics* in the dialogue on pages 208 and 209. In the dialogue are they *countable* or *uncountable*? Write them in the correct column.

Countable	Uncountable
tomatoes	*pasta*
_____	_____
_____	_____
_____	_____
_____	_____
_____	_____
_____	_____

 Check the answers

3 Look at the words in bold in the dialogue on pages 208–9. Answer the questions.

a *Some* is with a positive sentence. True/False?
b *Some* is with an offer. True/False?
c *Some* is with a negative sentence. True/False?
d Is *any* with positive or negative sentences?
e *Any* is with a question. True/False?
f Are *much/many* with a positive or a negative sentence?
g *Much/many* are with a question. True/False?
h *Much* is with countable nouns. True/False?
i *Many* is with countable nouns. True/False?
j *A lot of* is with countable and uncountable nouns. True/False?

 Check the answers

Form

4 Complete the table. Use ✔ or ✗.

	Countable	Uncountable	Positive	Negative	Questions
some	✔	a	b	✔	✔ offers
any	c	d	e	f	g
much	h	i	j	k	l
many	m	✗	n	o	p
a lot of	q	r	s	✔	✔

 Check the answers

Tip

Information is never plural.
I'd like some ~~informations~~/information.
Abstract nouns (e.g. *unemployment, love*) are never plural.
There is a lot of ~~unemployments~~/unemployment here.
~~Loves~~/Love is all you need.
Not Sure?
If you are not sure about *much* or *many*, use *a lot of*.

Common mistakes

5 Put ☑ for correct sentences and ☒ for incorrect sentences.

a We've got some apples. ☑
b We've got any apples. ☒
c How many money have you got? ☐
d How much money have you got? ☐
e I don't want some butter. ☐
f I don't want any butter. ☐
g There is many wine in the bottle. ☐
h There is a lot of wine in the bottle. ☐
i How many books have you got there? ☐

j How much books have you got there? ☐
k There's a lot of different cheeses. ☐
l There are a lot of different cheeses. ☐

✓ Check the answers

Practice

6 Countable – *a glass*, or uncountable – *glass*? Complete the sentences with *a* + noun (countable) or noun (uncountable).

a It's made of *glass*.

b Would you like *a glass* of wine?

c Would you like _____?

d I like _____

e Would you like _____?

f Would you like _____?

✓ Check the answers

7 Complete the sentences with *some* or *any*.

a I haven't got *any* milk.
b Would you like _____ tea?
c Is there _____ cheese in the sandwich?
d I bought _____ fruit.
e I can't see _____ fruit here.
f I saw _____ apples on the table.

✓ Check the answers

8 Choose *much*, *many* or *a lot of*. Sometimes two answers are correct.

a Chicago's got ~~much~~/a lot of/~~many~~ parks.

b Boston's got *much/many/a lot of* colleges.

c Is there *much/many/a lot of* unemployment in your country?

d Are there *much/many/a lot of* unemployed people in your country?

e Have you got *much/many/a lot of* homework?

f We haven't got *a lot of/much/many* eggs.

g We haven't got *much/many/a lot of* cheese.

 Check the answers

Now you

Write sentences about yourself and your town or country. Use ***much,
many, a lot of, some*** and ***any***.

a *I haven't got any* _____

b *I've got some* _____

c *My town/country has got* _____

d *There are a lot of* _____ *in my* _____

e *There aren't* _____ *in my* _____

➤ Unit 44 Articles
➤ Unit 45 Singular and plural nouns

48 | Comparison of adjectives – regular and irregular
■ James is older than his brother
■ His house is better

Meaning

1 Ryan and James are brothers. Read the text about the brothers and look at the information about them. Is Ryan A or B?

	A _____	B _____
Age	30	38
Height	1.7 metres	1.9 metres
Family	wife and four children	wife and two children
Salary	£30 000	£45 000
Car	Ford (1999)	Mercedes (2001)
House	3 bedrooms	5 bedrooms
	£200 000	£450 000

> Ryan is **younger** than his brother. He is also **shorter**. He is very busy – he has a big family. His family is **bigger** than James's. James is **happier** than Ryan. His salary is **higher**, his car is **more modern**, his house is **better** and **more valuable**.

 Check the answer

Form

The adjectives in bold in the text on page 214 are in the comparative form.

2 Complete the rules and form the comparative adjective.

a young   ⇨   young**er**
One syllable adjectives, add   **-er**   short   ⇨   _**shorter**_
b big   ⇨   big**ger**
One syllable adjectives with one vowel + one consonant
double the consonant and add   **-_ _**   thin   ⇨ _____
c happy   ⇨   happ**ier**
Two syllable adjectives with –y,
change –y to _   add   **-_ _**   easy   ⇨ _____
d modern   ⇨   **more** modern
Two or more syllables, use   _ _ _ _   valuable ⇨ _____
e good   ⇨   **better**
Some adjectives are irregular   bad   ⇨ **worse**
                                     far   ⇨ **farther or further**

✓ **Check the answers**

3 Look again at the text about the brothers and complete the table.

Ryan His family	is	younger bigger	**a** _____	his brother James's

✓ **Check the answer**

4 Put the adjectives in the correct column. Put them in the comparative form.

old	easy	bad	good	far	fast	lucky	comfortable
		~~nice~~	hot	wet	safe	boring	

+ -r	+ -er	✗ + ier	more...	double consonant	irregular
nicer ___ ___	___ ___	___ ___	___ ___	___ ___	___ ___ ___

✓ Check the answers

⚠ Common mistakes

5 Put ☑ for correct sentences and ☒ for incorrect sentences.

a Today is hotter than yesterday. ☑
b Today is more hot than yesterday. ☒
c He's taller that his sister. ☐
d He's taller than his sister. ☐
e Brazil is sunnier than Scotland. ☐
f Brazil is sunnyer than Scotland. ☐
g Rio is more poor than Brasilia. ☐
h Rio is poorer than Brasilia. ☐
i Chile is beautifuler than Argentina. ☐
j Chile is more beautiful than Argentina. ☐
k The weather is badder in London. ☐
l The weather is worse in London. ☐

✓ Check the answers

Tip

More or *–er*?
If you're not sure,
use *more*.

Practice

6 Make sentences about the country and the city. Use the words in the circle. Use the words more than once if necessary.

the country
healthier
cheaper   is   than
expensive   noisier
safer   the city
more

a *The country is cheaper than the city.*
b *The country is* _____
c *The city* _____
d _____
e _____

7 Write sentences about Oporto and Faro in Portugal. Use the comparative of the adjectives in the box.

| ~~big~~   small   sunny   hot   cool   cloudy |
| expensive   cheap |

	Oporto	**Faro**
Population	800,000	550,000
Hours of sunshine	1,680 per year	2,950 per year
Average temperature	16°C/61°F	20°C/68°F
Average hotel price	$200	$150

a *Oporto is bigger than Faro.*
b *Oporto is* _____ *than Faro.*
c _____

d   _____
e   _____
f   _____
g   _____
h   _____

✓ **Check the answers**

Now you

Compare your country with another country. Use comparative adjectives from this unit.

a *My country is* _____
b   _____
c   _____

49 Possessive adjectives
- This is my husband
- This is our daughter

Meaning

1 Sheila is looking at Rose's family photos. Read the conversation below and put these names in the correct place in the family tree:

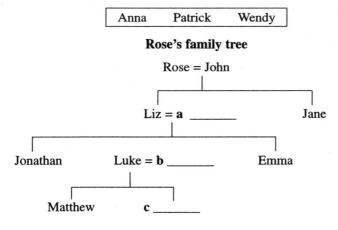

| Anna | Patrick | Wendy |

Rose's family tree

Rose = John

Liz = **a** _____   Jane

Jonathan   Luke = **b** _____   Emma

Matthew   **c** _____

Sheila	Rose, can I see **your** family photos?
Rose	Sure. This is **my** husband, John. He's a doctor. And this is **our** daughter, Liz, and that's **her** husband, Patrick. And this is a photo of **their** three children – **our** grandchildren – Jonathan, Emma and Luke. Luke's married – this is **his** wife, Wendy.

Sheila	So, is this a photo of **your** great grandchildren?
Rose	Yes, Matthew and Anna. Matthew and Anna have a dog. Look, that's **their** dog, Punch. And that's **its** little house in the garden. It's a very nice dog.

✔ **Check the answers**

Form

The words in **bold** in the dialogue on pages 219 and 220, are *possessive adjectives*.

Luke is married. He is married. This is his wife.

2 Look at the dialogue again and complete the table.

Pronoun	Possessive adjective
he	a *his*
I	b _____
you	c _____
she	d _____
it	e _____
we	f _____
they	g _____

✔ **Check the answers**

Tip

's
Luke is married. This is **his** wife. This is Luke**'s** wife.

its and it's
Punch is the dog. That's **its** house.   **its** = possessive adjective
It's a nice dog.   **it's** = it is

his and he's
This is Luke's wife. This is **his** wife.   **his** = possessive adjective
John's a doctor. **He's** a doctor.   **he's** = he is

⚠ **Common mistakes**

3 Put ☑ for correct sentences and ☒ for incorrect sentences.

a	His name's John.	☑	**i**	She's name is Rose	☐
b	Her name's John.	☒	**j**	Her name is Rose.	☐
c	He's a doctor.	☐	**k**	Your name's John.	☐
d	His a doctor.	☐	**l**	You're name's John.	☐
e	Her name is Anna.	☐	**m**	Where's John's house?	☐
f	Her name it's Anna.	☐	**n**	Where's Johns house?	☐
g	My fathers names John.	☐	**o**	What's your name?	☐
h	My father's name's John.	☐	**p**	What's you name?	☐

✓ **Check your answers**

Practice

4 Choose the correct word.

a ~~She~~/*Her* [flat/apartment] is on the first floor.

b *I/My* am 21 today.

c *He/His* birthday is tomorrow.

d This is *I/my* new car.

e *They/Their* house is at the end of the street.

f This is *Peter/Peter's* house.

g *Mary/Mary's* married.

h This is *our/we* new car.

i *She/Her* [has got/has] *my/me* car.

✓ **Check the answers**

5 Change the <u>underlined</u> words for a *possessive adjective*.

a Anna and ~~Anna's~~ *her* husband live in Cape Town.

b They have two children. <u>The children's</u> _____ names are Bill and Ben.

c They have a dog. <u>The dog's</u> _____ name is Chief.

d Andy's got five sons. <u>Andy's sons</u> _____ names are Dave, Ryan, Bill, Fred and Ricky.

e Andy and his sons live in a big house. <u>The house's</u> _____ front door is red.

✓ **Check the answers**

Now you

Draw four pictures. Describe them, using *possessive adjectives* and 's.

a *This is my house.*

b _____

c _____

d _____

e _____

50 Adverbs and adjectives
- You can eat your burger quickly
- The service is quick

Meaning

1 Answer the question about the texts below.

All the texts are about food. True/False?

I love *fast* food like McDonald's. The service is *good*. You can eat your burger **quickly** and go. It's so *easy*.

Well, the service is *good* at a *fast* food restaurant. You can order your food **quickly** and **easily**. But is the food *good* for you?

I do everything **fast**! I have a *fast* car. I drive **fast**, talk **fast**, work **fast**, walk **fast**, and eat **fast**! So I love *fast* food.

My husband's a *good* cook, a very *good* cook. He cooks pasta **well**, he makes *good* desserts, and he cleans up **well**!

My husband is a very *bad* cook. He cooks everything **badly**. He burns everything.

I'm a cook [in/at] a *fast* food restaurant. The work is very *hard*. I don't stop. I work very **hard** from the start of the day to the end of the day.

I woke up **late**. I had a *late* breakfast – people call it 'brunch' – breakfast and lunch together.

I woke up **early** – 4:00 A.M. – and I had an *early* breakfast. So I was really hungry at breakfast time…

 Check the answer

Adjectives have information about **nouns**: fast food

adjective noun

Adverbs have information about **verbs**: He cooks well

verb adverb

2 Look at the texts above. Are the adjectives or the adverbs in bold?

✓ Check the answer

Form

3 Complete the rules and form the adverbs.

a quick ⇨ quickly
Most adjectives add -_ _ bad ⇨ _____
b easy ⇨ easily
Adjectives with -y, change –y to -_
and add **-ly** heavy ⇨ _____
c fast ⇨ fast
Some words are adjectives and adverbs. early ⇨ _____
d good ⇨ well
'good' is irregular.

✓ Check the answers

4 Complete the table. The text on page 223 will help you.

Adjective	Adverb
a quick	*quickly*
b bad	_____
c _____	easily
d fast	_____
e _____	hard
f early	_____
g _____	late
h good	_____

✓ Check the answers

Tip

I speak   well   English.   ✗

| verb | adverb | object | ✗

I speak   English   well.   ✔

| verb | object | adverb | ✔

⚠ Common mistakes

5 Correct the mistakes.

a She speaks Russian very good.
She speaks Russian very well.

b He speaks Thai very fastly.

_____

c The service here is very quickly.

_____

d Mothers work very hardly at home.

_____

e The bus came lately.

_____

f Run quick – the train is here.

_____

✓ Check the answers

Practice

6 Adjective or Adverb? Underline the correct word.

a She works *hard/hardly*.
b English grammar is *easy/easily*.
c Shhhhhh! Speak *quiet/quietly*!
d Shhhhhh! You're so *noisy/noisily*!
e I always work *quick/quickly*.
f Be *quick/quickly*. We're late!
g She speaks Russian *good/well*.
h She's *good/well* at Russian.
i He's a *good/well* swimmer.

✓ Check the answers

7 Match a verb with an adverb. Sometimes two or more adverbs are possible.

a work

b walk

c wake up

d speak (Portuguese)

e know (someone)

late
fluently
well
hard
slowly
carefully

 Check the answers

8 Complete the sentences with an adverb. Use the adjectives in the box. Change the adjectives if necessary.

> ~~dangerous~~   careful   hard   good   bad   angry   fast

a He has a lot of accidents. He drives very *dangerously*.
b Ben Johnson ran the 100 [metres/meters] really _____
c Listen to the instructions _____
d It's dark. I can't see the road very _____
e The company isn't very good. They pay really _____
f She's always tired. She works too _____
g I lost her dictionary. She wasn't very happy and shouted at me really

_____

 Check the answers

Now you

Write about yourself. Use the adverbs:

  quickly   slowly   fast   well   badly

a *I speak* _____
b *I speak English* _____
c *I walk* _____
d *I don't drive* _____
e *I don't* _____
f *I* _____

> ➤ Unit 48 Comparison of adjectives – regular/irregular

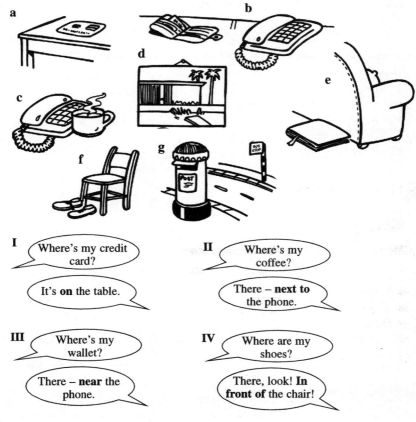

51 Prepositions of place
■ It's on the table
■ The shoes are in front of the chair

Meaning

1 Match the pictures with the conversations below.

I
Where's my credit card?

It's **on** the table.

II
Where's my coffee?

There – **next to** the phone.

III
Where's my wallet?

There – **near** the phone.

IV
Where are my shoes?

There, look! **In front of** the chair!

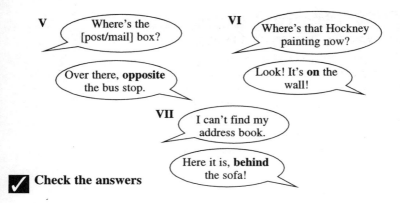

V Where's the [post/mail] box?

Over there, **opposite** the bus stop.

VI Where's that Hockney painting now?

Look! It's **on** the wall!

VII I can't find my address book.

Here it is, **behind** the sofa!

✓ **Check the answers**

Form

2 Look at the dialogues on pages 227 and 228. The words in bold are *prepositions*. Complete the table with the prepositions below.

behind	on	on	in front of	near	next to	opposite

Where's the parrot?		
It's	**a** _____	
	b _____	
	c _____	
	d _____	the box.
	e _____	
	f _____	
	g _____	the wall.

✓ **Check the answers**

⚠ Common mistakes

3 One preposition is incorrect. Underline the correct preposition.

a The lamp is <u>on</u>/*onto* the television.
b The lamp is *next*/*next to* the telephone.
c The lamp is *near from*/*near* the door.
d The lamp is *in front*/*in front of* the table.
e The lamp is *opposite*/*opposite from* the door.
f The lamp is *in*/*on* the wall.
g The lamp is *behind from*/*behind* the CD player.

✓ Check the answers

Practice

4 Look at the pictures. Underline the correct preposition.

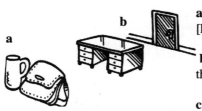

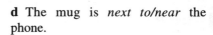

a The mug is <u>next to</u>/*in front* of the [handbag/purse].

b The desk is *opposite*/*in front of* the door.

c The keys are *in*/*on* the file.

d The mug is *next to*/*near* the phone.

e The picture is *on*/*next to* the mirror.

f The [diary/appointment book] is *on*/*behind* the desk.

 Check the answers

5 Look at the picture. Complete the sentences with the prepositions in the box.

| next to | next to | on | on | opposite | near | behind | in front of |

a The keys are *next to* the file.
b The file is _____ the keys.
c The mug is _____ the file.
d The plant is _____ the telephone.
e The telephone is _____ the plant.
f The computer is _____ the phone.
g There is a picture _____ the wall.
h There is a file _____ the desk.

✓ **Check the answers**

Now you

Write some sentences about your room. Where are the things in your room? Use prepositions to describe their locations.

a *There is a* _____
b *The* _____ *is on* _____
c *The* _____ *is in front of* _____
d _____ *on the wall.*
e _____
f _____
g _____

> Unit 52 Prepositions of time

52 Prepositions of time
- at 5:30 A.M.
- on Friday
- in the morning

Meaning

1 Match the questions and the answers.

a What time do you go to bed?

b Do you wake up early?

c What time of year do you see your family?

d When do you relax and go to the [cinema/movies]?

e When do you drink your first cup of coffee?

f What day of the week were you born?

Yes! **At** 5:30 A.M. usually.

At midnight – which is too late really.

[At/on] the weekend. That's when I see all the new films.

At Christmas – that's when we all get together.

On Friday, and I was two weeks late!

At breakfast time with a croissant.

 Check the answers

2 Match the questions and the answers.

a I hear you were born on the worst day of the year for birthdays....

b When did you get married?

c When was the first year you watched the Olympic Games?

d When's your next holiday?

e What time of day do you work best?

f When do you start [university/ college]?

That was **in** 1996. Donovan Bailey won gold in the 100 [metres/meters].

Yes, my birthday is **on** Christmas Day!

On June 17th – it was a sunny day.

In the [autumn/fall] – I'm studying history.

In August – I'm flying to Sydney.

In the morning. I feel awake then.

 Check the answers

3 Look at the questions and answers in exercises 1 and 2. The words in bold are prepositions. Find examples of the uses and write them in the table below.

Uses	Examples
At	
Times of the day Meal Times [Festivals/Holidays] Weekends Other	**a** *at 5:30 A.M.* **b** at_____ **c** _____ **d** _____ (British English only) *at night* *at the moment*
On	
Days Dates Other	**e** on _____ **f** _____ *on Monday morning/afternoon/evening/night*
In	
Years Parts of the day Seasons Months	**g** in _____ **h** _____ **i** _____ **j** _____

✔ Check the answers

Form

4 Complete the table. Use the prepositions in the box below.

on at in

Don't go	**a** _____	8 o'clock midday night Easter the moment dinner time
I'm busy	**b** _____	Wednesday March 5 New Year's Day Thursday afternoon
	c _____	May 2050 the winter the afternoon

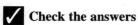 Check the answers

Tip

No **at, on,** or **in** with $\begin{cases} this \\ last \\ next \end{cases}$
this — What are you doing *this morning*?
last — I worked *last week*.
next — I'm free *next Monday*.

⚠ Common mistakes

5 Correct the mistakes.

a Come at Monday.
   Come on Monday.

b We leave the Thursday.

_____

c Come the Tuesday morning

_____

d I can't sleep in night

_____

e Come at the morning.

   _____

f Come on next Wednesday.

   _____

✓ **Check the answers**

Practice

6 Complete the information about holidays in Britain and the U.S.A.

a Most people don't work *[at/on]* the weekends.

b Most [shops/stores] open _____ Sunday.

c Many children open presents _____ Christmas Day.

d Some people go to church _____ midnight _____ Christmas Eve.

e St. Valentine's Day is _____ February 14th.

f There is a three or four day [holiday/vacation] _____ Easter.

✓ **Check the answers**

7 Complete the sentences with a preposition if necessary.

a Eleanor and I met ___–___ last Monday.

b We had lunch _____ Wednesday.

c We met _____ 1:30.

d We walked by the river _____ the afternoon.

e We looked at the stars _____ night.

f We met again _____ the weekend.

g She asked me to marry her _____ dinner time _____ Sunday evening.

h We're getting married _____ next week.

i The wedding will be _____ [29 February/February 29].

j _____ the moment we're very excited.

k Our honeymoon will be later _____ the summer.

✓ **Check the answers**

Now you

Answer the questions about you. Use prepositions and time words.

a What time do you go to bed?

   At _____

b What time do the [shops/stores] open in your country?

_____

c When do you go on [holiday/vacation]?

_____

d When do you go shopping?

_____

e When do you drink coffee?

_____

f When do you watch TV?

_____

g When was the last time you gave a present?

_____

h When was the last time you sent a card?

_____

i When do you have a special meal?

_____

j What month is your birthday?

_____

k What season were you born in?

_____

l What year were you born?

_____

➤ Unit 51 Prepositions of place

53 | Phrasal verbs – without objects
- I woke up at 5
- I got up at 6

Meaning

1 Read the short story and answer the question. One night someone is at home. A strange girl arrives...

How many people are in the bedroom at the end of the story?

> ### A short short story
>
> I was at home. It was late at night. I **sat down** and watched TV. I heard a noise and **looked up**. A girl **came in**. She said, 'Come with me.' I **got up** and went with her to my bedroom. She **went in**. I **went in**, too. Then the girl **went out** and shut the door. Suddenly it was very dark in the room and the door was locked...

✓ Check the answer

2 The verbs in bold are *phrasal verbs*. Match the phrasal verbs in the story with the pictures.

sat down _____ _____

d

e

f

_____   _____   _____

 Check the answers

Form

3 A *phrasal verb* is a verb + *in/out/up/down*, etc. For example *sit + down*, *go + out*. Make phrasal verbs for the pictures. Use a word from the box.

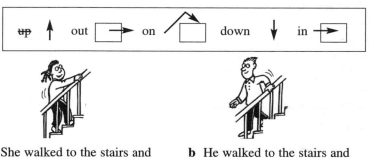

<table>
<tr><td>u̶p̶</td><td>↑</td><td>out</td><td>☐→</td><td>on</td><td>⟋☐</td><td>down</td><td>↓</td><td>in</td><td>→☐</td></tr>
</table>

a She walked to the stairs and went **up**.

b He walked to the stairs and went _____

c She went to the window and looked _____

d The bus arrived and he got

_____

e The taxi stopped and she got

_____

f When I came into the room,   **g** She went onto the balcony
he stood_____   and looked _____

h I was tired, went into the
bedroom and lay _____

i I opened the door and
walked _____

☑ **Check the answers**

Tip

There are thousands of phrasal verbs. Organize them by topic. For
example:

House and home	**[Transport/Transportation]**
come in	get in
go out	get on
get up	
sit down	

Practice

4 Complete the sentences with a word from the box.

~~up~~ down down down out up in on

a I looked ***up*** and saw an [aeroplane/airplane] in the sky.
b We arrived at John's house. He opened the door and we went _____.
c We went to the top of the Statue of Liberty in New York and looked
_____. The view below was fantastic.

d We went to the station and, when the first train arrived, we got _____ quickly.

e I found a free seat in the [cinema/movie theater] and sat _____.

f A police car arrived and three policeman got _____. They ran to the bank.

g The telephone rang. I got _____ and answered it.

h I went to my room and lay _____ on the bed.

✓ **Check the answers**

5 Complete the sentences with a verb from the box. Put the verb in the right form.

~~come~~	go	get	go	look	get	go

a I went out of the kitchen and opened the front door. Three cats *came* in from the street!

b I needed milk so I _____ out to go to the [shop/store].

c My taxi arrived. I took my luggage from the house and _____ in.

d The baby was crying upstairs so I _____ up to see her.

e I think I can hear a noise downstairs. Can you _____ down and look?

f Some people think it's polite to _____ up when someone comes in.

g There was a noise from the garden. I was downstairs and went to the window and _____ out.

✓ **Check the answers**

Now you

Write about what you did yesterday. Use phrasal verbs, for example, *come in, go out, get up.*

a *Yesterday I got up at* _____

b *I went* _____

c *I* _____

d *I* _____

➤ Unit 54 Phrasal verbs – with objects

54 Phrasal verbs – with objects
- He turned on the light
- He turned it on

Meaning

1 Read the short story and answer the questions. One night Peter is at home. A strange girl arrives...

There are two people in the bedroom at the end of the story. True/False?

A short short story

Peter came home. It was late at night. He **turned on** a light. The house was very dark. There was another light at the end of the hall. He **turned** it **on**. Peter was tired. He **sat down** and watched TV. He felt cold, very cold. There was a noise and he **looked up**. A strange girl in white **came in**. She said, 'Come with me.' Peter followed her to the bedroom. He **turned** the light **on**. Then the girl **went out** and shut the door. Suddenly there was no light. Someone **turned** it **off**. It was very dark, very cold and the door was locked...

 Check the answer

2 The verbs in bold are *phrasal verbs*. Some *phrasal verbs* have no object – 'He sat down.' Match the *phrasal verbs* in the story with the pictures. The *phrasal verbs* have no objects.

a

b

c

sat down _____ _____

d

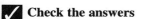

 Check the answers

3 Some *phrasal verbs* have objects: 'He turned on *the light*.' Match the phrasal verbs in the story with the pictures. The *phrasal verbs* have objects.

a   b

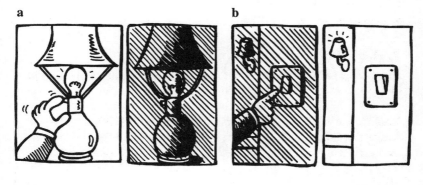

 Check the answers

Form

A phrasal verb is a verb + *in/out/up/down*, etc. For example, *sit* + *down*, *go* + *out*. You can write phrasal verbs with objects in three ways.

4 Look at the short story above and complete the sentences.

a He turned on _____
b He turned the light _____
c He turned _____ on.

 Check the answers

5 Write the sentence in three ways.

a He _____ off the light.
b He turned the light _____
c He turned _____

Tip

He turned on the light.
→ He turned it on. ✓
→ He turned ~~on it~~. ✗
Pronouns always come after *the verb*.

6 Match the pictures to the sentences with *phrasal verbs*.

I took the phone and [**rang up/called up**] Jean.

He **put** his shoes **on**.

It was a new word so I **looked** it **up** in the dictionary.

There was no smoking in the office so she **put out** her cigarette.

It was hot so she **took off** her coat.

He made a mistake so he **crossed** his name **out**.

She finished the book and **put** it **down**.

I dropped my keys and quickly **picked** them **up**.

✓ **Check the answers**

⚠ Common mistakes

7 One of the sentences below contains a mistake with a phrasal verb. Can you find it?

a They put on their caps.
b He picked up his pen and then put down it on the table.
c I found my jacket and put it on.

✓ **Check the answer**

Practice

8 Write the same sentence in three ways.

a She put the hat on.
  She put *on* the hat .
  She put *it* on.
b He _____ up the director.
  He _____ up.
  He _____ him _____
c She took _____ her clothes.
  She _____ off.
  She _____ her clothes _____
d He picked up _____
  He _____ the keys _____
  He _____

✓ **Check the answers**

9 Complete the sentences with a word from the box.

~~on~~   on   up   off   off

a He put *on* his coat.
b He wanted to read and turned _____ his bedroom light.
c He wanted to sleep so turned his bedroom light _____ .
d She called her friend _____ to tell her the news.
e She was hot with her coat on so she took it _____ .

✓ **Check the answers**

10 Complete the sentences with a verb from the box. Put the verb in the correct form.

~~pick~~	look	cross	put	put

a She dropped her bag and the porter *picked* it up.
b I arrived at the check-in desk at the airport and _____ my bags down.
c I didn't know the capital city of Peru so I _____ it up in an encyclopedia.
d You can't smoke on the train. Please _____ that cigarette out.
e I made a mistake with the English word and _____ it out.

✓ **Check the answers**

Now you

Write about you yesterday. Use phrasal verbs, for example, *turn on, turn off, put on, [ring up/call up], take off, look up.*

a *Yesterday I put on* _____
b *I [rang/called] up* _____
c *I* _____
d _____
e _____

> Unit 53 Phrasal verbs – without objects

Irregular verbs

Infinitive	Past Simple	Past Participle
be (am/is/are)	was/were	been
begin	began	begun
bite	bit	bitten
break	broke	broken
bring	brought	brought
build	built	built
buy	bought	bought
catch	caught	caught
choose	chose	chosen
come	came	come
cost	cost	cost
cut	cut	cut
do	did	done
draw	drew	drawn
drink	drank	drunk
drive	drove	driven
eat	ate	eaten
fall	fell	fallen
feel	felt	felt
find	found	found
fly	flew	flown
forget	forgot	forgotten
get	got	[got/gotten]
give	gave	given
go	went	gone
have	had	had
hear	heard	heard
hide	hid	hidden

hit	hit	hit
hold	held	held
hurt	hurt	hurt
keep	kept	kept
know	knew	known
leave	left	left
lend	lent	lent
lie*	lay	lain
light	lit	lit
lose	lost	lost
make	made	made
mean	meant	meant
meet	met	met
pay	paid	paid
put	put	put
read	read	read
ride	rode	ridden
ring	rang	rung
run	ran	run
say	said	said
see	saw	seen
sell	sold	sold
send	sent	sent
shine	shone	shone
shoot	shot	shot
show	showed	shown
shut	shut	shut
sing	sang	sung
sit	sat	sat
sleep	slept	slept
speak	spoke	spoken
spend	spent	spent
stand	stood	stood
steal	stole	stolen
swim	swam	swum
take	took	taken
teach	taught	taught
tear	tore	torn

tell	told	told
think	thought	thought
throw	threw	thrown
understand	understood	understood
wake	woke	woken
wear	wore	worn
win	won	won
write	wrote	written

*For example: to lie on a bed.

Irregular verbs in groups

No changes

Infinitive	Past Simple	Past participle
cost	cost	cost
cut	cut	cut
hit	hit	hit
hurt	hurt	hurt
put	put	put
shut	shut	shut

Past Simple and past participle the same

lend	lent	lent
send	sent	sent
spend	spent	spent

build	built	built

lose	lost	lost
shoot	shot	shot

get	got	[got/gotten]
light	lit	lit
sit	sat	sat

keep	kept	kept
sleep	slept	slept

feel	felt	felt
leave	left	left
meet	met	met

| mean | meant | meant |

bring	brought	brought
buy	bought	bought
think	thought	thought

| catch | caught | caught |
| teach | taught | taught |

| sell | sold | sold |
| tell | told | told |

find	found	found
have	had	had
hear	heard	heard
hold	held	held
make	made	made
pay	paid	paid
read	read	read
say	said	said

| stand | stood | stood |
| understand | understood | understood |

All different

Infinitive	Past Simple	Past participle
break	broke	broken
choose	chose	chosen
speak	spoke	spoken
steal	stole	stolen
wake	woke	woken

drive	drove	driven
ride	rode	ridden
write	wrote	written

bite	bit	bitten
hide	hid	hidden

eat	ate	eaten
fall	fell	fallen
forget	forgot	forgotten
give	gave	given
see	saw	seen
take	took	taken

know	knew	known
throw	threw	thrown
fly	flew	flown

draw	drew	drawn
show	showed	shown

wear	wore	worn
tear	tore	torn

begin	began	begun
drink	drank	drunk
swim	swam	swum

ring	rang	rung
sing	sang	sung

run	ran	ran

come	came	come

Grammar summaries

Tenses

Present Simple: *be*

Positive

I	am ('m)	
He She It	is ('s)	in New York
We You They	are ('re)	

'm, **'s** and **'re** are short forms or *contractions*. Use *contractions* in speaking and informal writing.

Negative

I	am not ('m not)	
He She It Emma	is not (isn't)	in the photograph
We You They	are not (aren't)	

n't is short for **not**. Use the short from in speaking and informal writing.

Question

Am	I	
Is	he she it Emma	in the photograph?
Are	we you they	

Present Simple: *there is/there are*

Positive

There	is 's	a problem
	are	problems

Negative

There	is not isn't	a letter
	are not aren't	44 letters

Question

Is		a lake	
	there		in the park?
Are		lakes	

Present Simple: *Full verbs*

Positive

I We You They Sumo wrestlers	eat have	lunch at 11:30 A.M. breakfast
He She It A sumo wrestler	eats has	

Negative

I We You They Sumo wrestlers	do not don't	eat lunch at 11:30 A.M. have breakfast
He She It A sumo wrestler	does not doesn't	

Question

Do	I we you they	shop online	?
Does	he she it	work well	

Meaning

Facts	In Singapore 90% of people live in apartments.
Routines and habits	A sumo wrestler gets up at 5:00 A.M.
What is generally true	The earth travels at 67,000 mph.

Present Simple with *frequency adverbs*

always	100%
usually	70%
often	60%
sometimes	30%
never	0%

I We You They	always usually often	eat meat buy a newspaper
He She It	sometimes never	eats meat buys a newspaper

Present Simple with *when*

When I	'm older, get older,	will you	love me make tea for me	?
		are you going to		
		I will	love you make tea for you	

Meaning

When + Present Simple = future meaning

The Imperative

Positive and negative

Go		[straight on/straight]			
Turn		left right			
Take		the	first street second street	on the	right left
Don't	go	[straight on/straight]			
	turn	left right			
	take	the	first street second street	on the	right left

Meaning

Instructions	First **boil** the water. Then **pour** it into the teapot.
Advice	**Don't go out** in Delhi alone at night.
Directions	**Turn** right at the traffic [lights/light].

Present Progressive

Positive and negative

I	am 'm	(not)	
He She Charlie	is	(not) (n't)	going to a jazz club
We You They	are		

Question

Am	I	
Is	he she Charlie	going to a jazz club?
Are	we you they	

Meaning

Action in progress now	She's busy. She's talking.
Future arrangements	I'm flying to Paris next week.

Past Simple: *be*

Positive			**Negative**			**Question**		
I He She It	was	OK	I He She It	was not wasn't	OK	Was	I he she it	OK?
We You They	were		We You They	weren't		Were	we you they	

Past Simple: *there is/there are*

Positive and negative

There	was	not n't	a population of 3.6 million then a Berlin Wall then
	were		1 million people in the city then millions of [mobile/cell] phones then

Question

Was		a [mobile/cell] phone in the room	
	there		?
Were		any [mobile/cell] phones in the room	

Past Simple: *Full verbs*

Regular verbs add **-d/-ed**:   live → lived, want → wanted
Irregular verbs can change: give → gave

Positive and negative

I He She The robber We You They The cashiers	wanted money gave $1,000 to the thief	
	didn't	want money give $1,000 to the thief

Question

Did	I he she the robber we you they the robbers	want	money?
		give	$1,000

Going to future

Positive and negative

I	am 'm	(not)		
He She It	is	(not) (n't)	going to	have a party
We You They	are			stay at home

Question

Are	we you they	going to	buy a house?
Is	he she		have a holiday?

[Have got/Have]

British English

Positive and negative

(Americans use the contraction.)

I We You They	have (n't) 've	got	a swimming pool a television
He She It	has (n't) 's		

Question

Note: Both British and American speakers use 'Have/has... got...?'.

Have	I we you they	got	a swimming pool a television	?
Has	he she it			

American English

Positive

I We You They	have	a car
He She It	has	a television

Negative

I We You They	don't	have	a television
He She It	doesn't		

Question

Do	I we you they			
		have	a television	?
Does	he she it			

First Conditional

If	we look after the planet, we don't look after the planet,	we people	will	live die

Present Perfect Simple

Positive, negative and question

I We You They	have			
		n't not	been on the beach	
He She It	has		[travelled/traveled] a lot	
Have	I we you they		been on the beach	?
Has	he she it		[travelled/traveled] a lot	

Positive, negative and question

I We You They	have	not n't					
He She It	has		worked	for	three months two years a long time ten minutes	
Have	I we you they			since	January 5 o'clock he was a boy	?
Has	he she it					

Meaning

Indefinite past I've [travelled/traveled] a lot.
Past to present situation I've worked for 2 years.

Present Perfect Progressive

Positive and negative

I We You They	have	n't not	been	living here	for 10 years
He She It	has				since 1999

Question

Have	I we you they			for 10 years	
		been	living here		?
Has	he she it			since 1999	

Used to do

Positive, negative and question

I He She It We You They	used to		work wear miniskirts
	didn't	use to	

Question

Did	I he she it we you they	use to	work wear miniskirts	?

Meaning

Past habit   She used to wear miniskirts but she doesn't now.

Past Progressive

Positive, negative and question

I He She It	was	(not) (n't)	swimming in the sea
We You They	were		
Was	I he she it	swimming in the sea?	
Were	we you they		

Modal verbs

Will

Positive and negative

He She It We You They	will 'll will not won't	lose win
I	'll	answer the phone carry your bag

Question

Will	I he she it we you they	win?

Meaning

Prediction	It will rain.
Decisions made now	I'll answer the phone.
Offer to help	I'll carry it.

Would like

I'd like	a coffee Swiss francs		
	to	have coffee eat lunch	

Would you like	a coffee Swiss francs		?
	to	have coffee eat lunch	

Meaning

Requests	I'd like a coffee. I'd like to have a coffee.
Offers	Would you like a coffee? Would you like to have a coffee?

Can/Could

Positive, negative and question

I He She It We You They	can cannot can't could couldn't	fly swim	
Can Could	I he she it		?

Can't is short for **cannot**. **Can't** is for informal written and spoken English.

Meaning

Ability   I can swim.

Can I...?/Could I...?/[Is it all right if/may]...?

Can I Could I [Is it all right if I/may I]	use the phone? borrow your dictionary?

Can you Could you	pass me the sugar? help me?

Meaning

Request for permission	Can I use the phone?
A more polite request for permission	Could I use the phone?
Very polite request for permission	[Is it all right if/May] I use the phone?
Request	Can you pass the sugar?
A more polite request	Could you pass the sugar?

Might

Positive and negative

I He She It We You They	might	(not)	arrive late

Meaning
Possibility It might rain.

Shall...?

Shall	I we	help you? go now?

Meaning

Offer Shall I help you?
Suggestion Shall we go now?

Must

Positive and negative

I He She It We You They	must	(not) (n't)	go now be late

Meaning

Obligation   I must go. (*The speaker thinks it is necessary to go.*)
                  I mustn't be late. (*The speaker thinks it is important not to be late.*)

Have to/had to

Present: positive and negative

I We You They	have to don't have to	go wait
He She It	has to doesn't have to	

Past: positive and negative

I He She It They We You	had to didn't have to	go wait

Question

Do	I/you/we/they	have to	go?
Does	he/she/it		
Did	I/we/you/they he/she/it		

Meaning

I have to go.	(*Another person thinks it is necessary for me to go.*)
I don't have to go.	(*It is not necessary for me to go.*)
I had to go.	(*It was necessary for me to go.*)
I didn't have to go.	(*It wasn't necessary for me to go.*)

Should/'d better

Positive, negative and question

I He She It We You They	should	(n't)	eat fruit exercise
	'd better	(not)	
Should	I he she it we you they		eat fruit? exercise?

Meaning

Advice   You should eat fruit.
        You shouldn't eat fruit.
        You'd better exercise.
        You'd better not exercise.

'd better is for one action or one situation, not for things in general.

Drivers 'd better wear seat belts. The situation is general so: Drivers should wear seat belts.

Questions

Yes/no questions with *be*

Am Was	I	
Is Was	he she It	in the photo ?
Are Were	we you they	

Yes/no questions: with *do*

Present Simple

Do	I we you they	
Does	he she it	look OK ?

Past Simple

Did	I he she it we you they	look OK?

Wh- questions: with *do* and *be*

When Where Who How What Why Which Whose	do did	you	play see	?

When Where Who How What Why Which Whose	is was	it he	?

Questions: subject and object

Subject questions

Who	shot the man? saw the man?

Object questions

[Who/ Whom]	did	you	shoot? see?

Echo questions

be	→	*am/is/are/was/were*
She**'s** He **isn't** They**'re** You**'re** He **wasn't** They **were**	late.	**Is** she? **Isn't** he? **Are** they? **Am** I? **Wasn't** he? **Were** they?

full verb	→	*do/does/did*
She **works** He **doesn't** I **work** They **worked**	here.	**Does** she? **Doesn't** he? **Do** you? **Did** they?

modal verb	→	modal verb
She **can** They **couldn't**	swim.	**Can** she? **Couldn't** they?

Meaning

Show interest or surprise   A I was late today. **B** Were you?

Embedded questions

Question		**Embedded Question**
Is he in his office?	→	Can you tell me **if** he is in his office?
Does the train leave at 2:00?	→	Can you tell me **if** the train leaves at 2:00?
When does the train leave?	→	Can you tell me when the train leaves ?

Meaning

Polite question   Could you tell me where the station is, please?

Verbs + gerund/infinitive

Verb + gerund		Verb + infinitive	
I like I love I enjoy I hate I finished I stopped	cook**ing**	I'd like I hope I want I promised I decided	**to go** to the U.S.A.

Meaning

Verb + infinitive
Often the main verb happens first.

I want *to go*. 'Want' happens before 'go'.

Verb + gerund
Often the main verb happens second.

It stopped *raining*. 'stopped' happened after 'raining'.

Articles and nouns

Indefinite article: *a* and *an*

This is a spelling and pronunciation rule.

a before consonant sounds:	a thief, a town, a basket, a hotel a university (pronounced 'yuniversity'), a European city (pronounced 'yeuropean')
an before vowel *sounds*	an apple, an ice cube an hour (pronounced 'our') an M.A. (pronounced 'emmay')

Indefinite article: uses

One of many	I saw *a* thief in *a* supermarket.
Jobs	My father's *a* teacher.
First mention	*A* thief walked into *a* supermarket.

Definite article: uses

Superlative adjectives	*The* biggest supermarket in Southampton.
Only one	*The* queen of England.
Second mention	A thief walked into a supermarket. I watched *the* thief take a trolley.

Zero article: uses

Streets	I live in Russell Street.
Towns	Russell Street is in Southampton.
Countries	Southampton is a city in England.
General meaning	I like rock music. I hate examinations. Flowers are beautiful. Courage is important.
Meals	What do you want for breakfast? Dinner is ready.
Common places with prepositions	I'm going to work, you're going to school, Dad's in prison, Pete's in bed, and the cat's at home.
Sports and games	I like chess, rugby and skiing.
Academic subjects	English is easy. Physics and mathematics are difficult.

Nouns: singular and plural

Examples:

Singular	Plural
person	people
woman	women
man	men
child	children
church	churches
house	houses
factory	factories
bus	buses
[lorry/truck]	[lorries/trucks]
car	cars

Spelling

After most nouns add **-s**	car → cars, week → weeks
After consonant + -y, add **-ies**	story → stories, factory → factories
After vowel + -y, add **-s**	holiday → holidays, boy → boys
After -s, add **-es**	dish → dishes, wish → wishes
After -ch, add **-es**	church → churches, watch → watches
After -s, add **-es**	kiss → kisses, bus → buses
After -x, add **-es**	box → boxes, fox → foxes
After -f, add **-ves**	shelf → shelves, loaf → loaves
After -fe, add **-ves**	wife → wives, life → lives
After vowel + -o, add **-s**	radio → radios, video → videos
After consonant + -o, add **-es**	tomato → tomatoes, potato → potatoes
Two irregular nouns with consonant + -o	photo → photos, piano → pianos

Irregular plurals

man	→	men
woman	→	women
child	→	children
person	→	people
tooth	→	teeth
foot	→	feet
sheep	→	sheep
fish	→	fish
mouse	→	mice

Pronouns

Example:

There is a phone call for *Mr. Evans*. <u>He</u> doesn't work here now. Are you sure the call's for **him**?

Mr. Evans	– noun
<u>He</u>	– subject pronoun
him	– object pronoun

Noun	Subject pronoun	Object pronoun
John	I	me
Peter	you	you
Mr. Evans	he	him
Mary	she	her
my car	it	it
my cars	they	them
the children	they	them
Jane and I	we	us

Nouns: countable and uncountable

Countable nouns
a drink/drinks
a dollar/dollars
an egg/eggs

Uncountable nouns
water
money
food

Some nouns are countable (The *cheeses* they make in France) and uncountable (I like *cheese*).

Some nouns are usually only uncountable (*information* NOT *informations*). Other examples: advice, weather, furniture, accommodation.

Some and *any*

Some

Positive sentences	I'd like some tea.
	There are some cups on the table.
Offers	Would you like some tea?

Any

Negative sentences	I don't want any tea.
	There aren't any cups on the table.
Questions	Have you got any tea?
	Are there any cups on the table?

Much and *many*

Much

Uncountable nouns in questions	Have you got much cash with you?
Uncountable nouns in negative sentences	I haven't got much cash with me.

Many

Countable nouns in questions	Have you got many apples?
Countable nouns in negative sentences	We haven't got many apples.

a lot of

With countable nouns	We've got a lot of apples.
With uncountable nouns	I've got a lot of cash with me.

Adjectives

Comparative adjectives

Examples:

Jane is young*er than* John.
Tokyo is bigg*er than* Madrid.
Gold is *more* expensive *than* silver.

Rules

One syllable adjectives add **-er**	young → young**er**, short → short**er**
One syllable adjectives with one vowel + one consonant, double the consonant and add **-er**	big → big**ger**, thin → thin**ner**
Two syllable adjectives with -y, change –y to **-i** and add **-er**	happy → happ**ier**, easy → eas**ier**
Two or more syllables use **more**	valuable → **more** valuable modern → **more** modern
Some adjectives are irregular	bad → **worse**, good → **better** far → **further** or **farther**

Possessive adjectives

Example:

Luke is married. He is married. This is **his** wife.

Luke – noun
he – pronoun
his – possessive adjective

Pronoun	Possessive adjective
he	his
I	my
you	your
she	her
it	its
we	our
they	their

's

Luke is married. This is **his** wife. This is Luke**'s** wife.

its and *it's*

Punch is the dog. That's **its** house. **its** = *possessive adjective*
It's a nice dog. **it's** = *it is*

his and *he's*

This is Luke's wife. This is **his** wife. **his** = *possessive adjective*
John's a doctor. **He's** a doctor. **he's** = *he is*

Adverbs

Example:

I like fast food.
Adjectives have information about nouns:

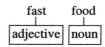

fast food
adjective noun

Example:

I woke up late.

Adverbs have information about verbs: He cooks   well

| verb | adverb |

Rules to make adverbs from adjectives

Most adjectives add **-ly**	bad → bad**ly**, quick → quick**ly**
Adjectives with -y, change -y to **-i** and add **-ly**	easy → eas**ily**, heavy → heav**ily**
Some words are adjectives and adverbs	fast → **fast**, early → **early**
Good is irregular	good → **well**

Prepositions

Prepositions of place

Where's the parrot?		
It's	**a** on **b** near **c** next to **d** behind **e** opposite **f** in front of	the box.
	g on	the wall.

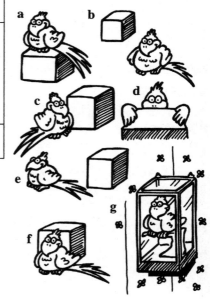

Prepositions of time

Uses	Examples
At	
Clock time	at 5:30 A.M., at midnight
Meal times	at lunch time, at breakfast time
[Festivals/Holidays]	at Christmas, at Easter, at Ramadan
Weekends	at the weekend (British English only)
Other	at night
	at the moment
On	
Days	on Monday, on Sunday
Dates	on March 5th, on January 2nd
Weekends	on the weekend (American English only)
Other	on Monday morning/afternoon/evening/night
In	
Years	in 2001, in 1842
Parts of the day	in the morning, in the afternoon, in the evening
Seasons	in the summer, in the winter
Months	in January, in August

There is no preposition with *this, last* or *next.*

Examples:

What are you doing *this morning*? I worked *last week.* I'm free *next Monday.*

Phrasal verbs

A *phrasal verb* is a verb + *in/out/up/down/on,* etc. For example, sit + down, go + out.

Examples:

She *walked in* and *sat down.*
I *stood up* and *went out.*

Some *phrasal verbs* have objects.

Examples:

She *put on* her coat.

You can write *phrasal verbs* with objects in three ways.

She put on her coat.
She put her coat on.
She put it on.

She put on it. ✗

Pronouns always come *after* the verb.

Key to the exercises

Unit 1

1 a I'm from the U.S.A. My name's Doug. **b** We're thirty-three years old. **c** It's famous and it's in New York. **d** You're in room 3, the elementary class. **e** He's hungry. **f** They're Australian. **g** She's Australian.

2 a 'm **b** 's **c** 're

3 a am **b** is **c** is **d** is **e** are **f** are **g** are

4 a are **b** are **c** is **d** is **e** is **f** is **g** 'm **h** are **i** 're **j** is **k** 's **l** 's

5 a He's English. **b** Her name's Emma. **c** They're from New York. **d** My car's very new. **e** You're a teacher. **f** I'm Japanese. **g** She's a very good teacher. **h** We're from Tokyo.

Unit 2

1 a v **b** vi **c** iii **d** i **e** ii **f** iv

2 a am **b** he **c** it **d** are

3 a 'm **b** not **c** isn't **d** aren't

4 is not

5 a I'm not from Iceland. **b** Are you German? **c** They're not happy. **d** She isn't short. **e** Is he your boyfriend? **f** I'm not in the photograph. **g** We aren't happy. **h** You aren't French.

6 a Paris isn't the capital of Germany. **b** I'm hungry./I'm not hungry. **c** Luxembourg isn't a big country. **d** London isn't in France. **e** Gold isn't cheap. **f** Boxing is dangerous. **g** Oranges aren't vegetables. **h** I'm not Irish. **i** Potatoes are vegetables. **j** We aren't from Mars. **k** Charles is/isn't the king of England. **l** Al Gore is/isn't the U.S. president.

7 a Are we late? **b** Are we at the right hotel? **c** Are you French? **d** Are you Swiss? **e** Is French your first language? **f** Is it your cat in the photograph? **g** Is your wife Swiss? **h** Is she French? **i** Are they your children? **j** Are they twins?

8 a am **b** 'm not **c** she is **d** she isn't **e** it is **f** it isn't **g** we are **h** we aren't **i** they are **j** they aren't

9 a Yes, it is. **b** No, it isn't. **c** No, I'm not. **d** Yes, I am. **e** No, he isn't. **f** No, she isn't. **g** Yes, they are. **h** No, they aren't. **i** Yes, he is. **j** Yes, he is. **k** No, we aren't. **l** Yes, we are.

Unit 3

1 a false **b** true

2 a singular nouns **b** plural nouns

3 a is **b** are **c** is **d** isn't **e** aren't

4 a There is/'s a book on the table. **b** There are no volcanoes in England. **c** There are palm trees in Los Angeles. **d** There is/'s a car in the street.

5 a There are 12 months in a year. **b** There is 1 vowel in the word 'March'. **c** There are 7 days in a week. **d** There are 30 days in April. **e** There is 1 sun in the solar system.

Unit 4

1 a Yes, there is. **b** No, there aren't. **c** Yes, there are. **d** No, there isn't.

2 a true **b** true

3 a is **b** are **c** there **d** isn't **e** are **f** there **g** aren't

4 a Are there people on the moon? **b** No, there aren't. **c** Is there an American flag on the moon? **d** Yes, there is.

5 a Is there pasta in the fridge? **b** Is there cheese in the fridge? **c** Are there onions in the fridge? **d** Are there potatoes in the fridge?

6 a Is there a bus to the airport? **b** Are there trains after midnight? **c** Are there cheap tickets at weekends? **d** Are there taxis outside Central Station?

Unit 5

1 c a prison
2 a routines and habits
3 a work **b** don't **c** pays **d** doesn't
4 a ✗ **b** ✓ **c** ✗ **d** ✓ **e** ✗ **f** ✓ **g** ✗ **h** ✓ **i** ✗ **j** ✓ **k** ✗ **l** ✓ **m** ✗ **n** ✓ **o** ✗ **p** ✓ **q** ✓ **r** ✗
5 a People don't live on Mars. **b** Kangaroos don't walk backwards. **c** Elephants don't jump. **d** A snake doesn't close its eyes. **e** A male mosquito doesn't bite. **f** The sun doesn't go around the earth.
6 a don't smoke **b** doesn't smoke **c** don't smoke **d** don't see **e** don't understand
7 a goes **b** don't eat **c** don't tell **d** doesn't grow **e** rises **f** works **g** don't believe **h** don't live

Unit 6

1 a nothing
2 Yes
3 a the earth
4 a Yes **b** No **c** Yes **d** Yes
5 a what is generally true **b** routines and habits **c** facts
6 a Yes **b** No **c** No **d** No **e** No
7 a eat **b** have **c** eats **d** has
8 a trains **b** does **c** cries **d** buys **e** rushes **f** catches **g** misses **h** buzzes **i** relaxes **j** has **k** is
9 a ✓ **b** ✗ **c** ✗ **d** ✓ **e** ✓ **f** ✗ **g** ✗ **h** ✓ **i** ✓ **j** ✗ **k** ✓ **l** ✗ **m** ✗ **n** ✓ **o** ✓ **p** ✗
10 a studies **b** says, eats **c** finishes **d** goes **e** relaxes, watches **f** kisses **g** fizzes
11 a watches TV for 12 years **b** drink 73 billion cups of tea **c** lose 50–100 hairs **d** drinks 23 million Coca-Colas **e** serve 1 million people
12 a sleep **b** sleeps **c** has **d** sleeps **e** sleeps **f** have **g** are **h** go **i** falls **j** relaxes **k** are **l** move **m** dream
13 a walk **b** do **c** open **d** have **e** cooks **f** goes **g** drives **h** gets

Unit 7

1 a false **b** false
2 a do **b** does **c** do **d** does **e** don't **f** doesn't **g** Where
3 a Does she like shopping? **b** Do they spend a lot of money? **c** When do you shop? **d** Do you buy milk in the supermarket? **e** Does she

spend a lot? **f** When does he go to the supermarket?
4 a do what you do to me? **b** rain on me? **c** me…now that I can dance? **d** do you, do you want to dance?
5 a In Hong Kong. **b** No, I don't. **c** He's from Paris. **d** Yes, in the next street. **e** No, you don't. **f** 8:30. **g** Yes, he does.
6 a What time do you get up? **b** Do you have a shower or a bath? **c** Do you eat breakfast? **d** What do you have for lunch? **e** When do you finish work? **f** What do you do in the evenings? **g** Do you read in bed?
7 a Does David like cooking? **b** Does Sally speak Russian? **c** Does Sally eat meat? **d** Do David and Sally smoke? **e** Do David and Sally drink?
8 a Yes, he does. **b** No, she doesn't. **c** Yes, he does. **d** No, he doesn't. **e** No, she doesn't.
9 a Where do you live? **b** What time do you get up? **c** Where does your family live? **d** Where does your sister work? **e** What does your brother do?

Unit 8

1 a E **b** B **c** A **d** D **e** C
2 a always **b** usually **c** often **d** sometimes **e** never
3 a present simple **b** yes **c** before **d** after **e** after
4 a She always goes to the gym. **b** They don't always eat salad. **c** I never go to the [theatre/theater]. **d** We usually go by bus.
5 a We always go to Italy in August. **b** We sometimes drive there. **c** We often stay on a campsite. **d** The children never come with us. **e** We usually spend one week there.
6 a always eat breakfast. **b** never eats breakfast. **c** sometimes eats breakfast. **d** usually go shopping. **e** never goes shopping. **f** often goes shopping. **g** usually do the dishes. **h** never does the dishes. **i** often does the dishes.

Unit 9

1 a husband talking to his wife
2 a present simple **b** true **c** false **d** future **e** future **f** future **g** true
3 a will **b** get **c** won't **d** make **e** care
4 a When I am in London next week, I'm

going to visit The British Museum. **b** When I arrive at the station later, I'll phone you. **5 a** when I'm 64? **b** it will be forever. **c** I'm going to hold you tight.
6 a 'll phone, get **b** 'll tell, come **c** 'll wait, are **d** finish **e** arrive, 'll send

Unit 10

1 Yes
2 True
3 a turn **b** take **c** don't **d** take **4 a** Advice **b** Directions **c** Instructions
5 a Don't go out alone at night. **b** Go by bus. **c** Don't wait here. **d** Don't go [straight on/straight].
6 a go, Daddy, please come home. **b** with me because you're playing with fire **c** don't go… **d** me this way
7 a Paint a picture. **b** Write a novel. **c** Construct a ten-lane [motorway/highway]. **d** Direct a film. **e** Build a bridge.
8 a Don't drink alcohol. **b** Eat fresh fruit. **c** Don't eat red meat. **d** Sleep 7–8 hours.

Unit 11

1 a Yes **b** No
2 a present progressive **b** future **c** arrangement **d** decision from the past
3 a 'm **b** is **c** are **d** are
4 a I'm going out. **b** Are you watching the [match/game] tomorrow? **c** She isn't coming to the party next week. **d** Sorry, I'm going to John's house.
5 c e a d b f
6 a Are you leaving at 3? **b** We aren't flying to Paris on Friday. **c** When are they arriving? **d** I'm working all next week. **e** Your taxi's arriving soon. **f** How is she travelling to LA?
7 a are you doing **b** going to **c** I'm going to the [cinema/movies].

Unit 12

1 e nobody
2 a true **b** false
3 a 'm **b** is **c** are **d** n't **e** n't
4 a ing, working **b** -e, writing **c** -y, dying **d** stopping **e** beginning
5 a Look – she's coming. **b** I'm writing a letter now. **c** You're running too fast. **d** The

cat's sleeping. **e** They are not listening to me. **f** I'm not doing my homework at the moment.
6 a sailing **b** blowing in the wind **c** of a white Christmas **d** is give peace a chance **e** 's leaving home, bye, bye **f** strawberry fields
7 a She's laughing. **b** She isn't laughing. **c** I'm laughing. **d** I'm not laughing.
8 a is sitting **b** is reading **c** is playing **d** doing **e** is working **f** am enjoying **g** are doing

Unit 13

1 a works as a film director, lives in Los Angeles, makes one film every year **b** directing a new film, working in Delhi
2 a Peter lives, he makes **b** He's working **c** present simple for something permanent, present progressive for something temporary
3 a I work for a computer company. **b** Looking for my dictionary. **c** In Bombay. **d** In a hotel for a moment.
4

The *Present Simple* is for habits routines permanent things	The *Present Progressive* is for actions now temporary things

5 a Where do you usually work? **b** She goes swimming every day. **c** He's speaking Polish/He speaks Polish. **d** They don't like football. **e** Wait – I'm coming. **f** Look – he's walking very fast. **g** I'm driving to the airport at the moment. **h** We don't eat fish. **i** What are you doing there? **j** Jean is busy – she's [having/taking] a bath.
6 a Do you eat meat? **b** How do you do? **c** Are you eating meat? **d** What do you do? **e** What are you doing? **f** It's raining. **g** He's watching TV. **h** What language are you speaking? **i** Yes, I'm not listening to it. **j** The sun is shining.
7 a do you speak **b** is having **c** is playing **d** do you get up **e** is ringing **f** is doing **g** do not watch

Unit 14

1 a A **b** B
2 a was **b** were **c** wasn't **d** Was **e** Were
3 a Were you outside the [cinema/movies]?

b She was not in the car. **c** They were outside the bank. **d** I wasn't in the car. **e** My wife and I were in the back of the car. **f** Were the people in the car men or women?

4 a Were you late? **b** Was the boss late? **c** Were the e-mails late? **d** I wasn't late. **e** The boss wasn't late. **f** The e-mails weren't late. **g** The boss was late. **h** The e-mails were late. **i** I was late. **j** Was I late?

5 a was, was **b** was, was **c** was **d** were **e** were **f** was **g** was

6 a were **b** was **c** wasn't **d** wasn't **e** weren't **f** wasn't **g** wasn't **h** was **i** wasn't

Unit 15

1 a II **b** I **c** III

2 a was **b** were **c** n't **d** was **e** were

3 a There were thousands of people in Rio de Janeiro. **b** Were there any mobile phones in New Zealand in 1990? **c** There were not any videos before 1965.

4 a there wasn't **b** were there, there weren't **c** there was **d** there weren't **e** were there **f** there was, there wasn't **g** there was **h** there weren't

5 a weren't **b** wasn't **c** were **d** were **e** wasn't **f** were **g** weren't **h** were

Unit 16

1 No

2 a handed **b** asked **c** arrived **d** noticed **e** hurried **f** travelled **g** preferred **h** planned

3 Yes

4 a -ed, played **b** -d, saved **c** -i, studied **d** -l, cancelled **e** consonant, regretted **f** consonant, stopped

5 a lived **b** played **c** swallowed **d** terrified **e** walked **f** played

6 a travelled **b** preferred **c** robbed, pulled, started

Unit 17

1 a The child's mother filled in the form.

2 No

3 offered, filled, replied, wrote, gave, was, said, made,

4 Yes

5 a did **b** drank **c** flew **d** went **e** had **f** left **g** ran **h** saw **i** spent **j** swam **k** took

6 a leave, left **b** spend, spent **c** write, wrote **d** drink, drank

7 a ✗ **b** ✓ **c** ✓ **d** ✗ **e** ✗ **f** ✓

8 a swam **b** drank **c** spent **d** saw **e** took **f** flew **g** left **h** had

Unit 18

1 d nothing

2 a gave **b** give **c** didn't **d** want **e** did

3 a true **b** true **c** She didn't arrive. **d** He didn't leave. **e** Did they go?

4 a I didn't come. **b** He didn't arrive. **c** She didn't like tea. **d** Did we buy it here? **e** Did they live in Scotland. **f** They didn't see me.

5 a went **b** met **c** left **d** saw **e** began **f** arrived

6 a Prince Charles didn't become king of England in 1999. **b** The Niagara Falls in Canada froze completely in 1925. **c** Napoleon Bonaparte designed the Italian flag. **d** The U.S.A. didn't have a national anthem before 1931. **e** The *Titanic* didn't sink in 1955. **f** The Second World War didn't end in 1944.

7 a Where did you go for your last [holiday/vacation]? **b** Did you go by plane? **c** How much did the [holiday/vacation] cost? **d** When did you get back? **e** Did you have a good time?

8 a did you go **b** did you stay **c** did you **d** were there **e** what did you

9 a I watched TV./I didn't watch TV. **b** I got up before 6:00 A.M./I didn't get up before 6:00 A.M. **c** I spoke English./I didn't speak English. **d** I ate meat./I didn't eat meat.

Unit 19

1 Plans for retirement **c** Plans for lottery money **a** Plans for a [holiday/vacation] **b**

2 a True **b** True **c** False

3 a 'm **b** 's **c** 're **d** to **e** are **f** is **g** they **h** going **i** going **j** to

4 a I'm not going to watch TV tonight. **b** She's going to write a letter. **c** We're going to fly to Paris on Saturday. **d** They are not going to leave today. **e** Are you going to visit your parents? **f** What are you going to do [at/on] the weekend?

5 a I'm going to study. **b** She is not going to study. **c** She's going to study. **d** I'm not going to study. **e** Is she going to study?

6 a Are you going to fly to Paris? **b** We're going to eat breakfast. **c** Are they going to leave now? **d** He isn't going to go to school. **7 a** watch TV **b** going to [have/take] a bath **c** They're going to go to the [cinema/movies]. **d** It's going to go to sleep./It's going to sleep. **e** He isn't going to have/drink a cup of coffee. **f** She isn't going to play the piano. **g** They aren't going to buy dresses/clothes.

Unit 20

1 a II **b** I **c** III
2 a Possessions **b** Availability **c** Possessions **d** Availability
3 a they **b** 've **c** television **d** has **e** he
4 a you **b** has **c** swimming pool **d** do **e** she
5 a ✓ **b** ✗ **c** ✗ **d** ✓ **e** ✗ **f** ✓ **g** ✗ **h** ✓ **i** ✗ **j** ✓
6 a has got credit cards **b** hasn't got credit cards **c** haven't got/have got credit cards **d** hasn't got a house **e** has got a house **f** have got/ haven't got a house **g** have got a car **h** have got/haven't got a car
7 a Have they got a bar? **b** Has the hotel got a bar? **c** Has Max got a camera? **d** Have you got a camera? **e** Have you got a hotel? **f** Has Max got a hotel? **g** Has Max got a bar? **h** Have you got a bar?
8 a have **b** doesn't have **c** don't have **d** has **e** has **f** don't have **g** don't have

Unit 21

1 a True **b** False
2 a future **b** possible **c** possible
3 a *Present Simple* **b** *Future Simple* with *will* **c** Yes **d** No
4 a will **b** will **c** won't **d** will
5 a ✗ **b** ✓ **c** ✗ **d** ✓ **e** ✓ **f** ✗
6 a if **b** if **c** when **d** when **e** when **f** if
7 a will you make an omelette? **b** if I buy the flour **c** will you wash up? **d** if you bake it for three hours? **e** there won't be anything to eat
8 a if, will **b** if, will **c** will, if, will
9 a Will you pass your exams if you work hard? **b** If you pass your exams, you will go to college. **c** If I go to college, I will study history.

Unit 22

1 a II **b** I
2 a past to present
3 a Yes **b** Yes **c** Yes
4 a Yes **b** Yes
5 a Yes **b** Yes
6 a period of time **b** starting time
7 a 've **b** 's **c** worked **d** for **e** since **f** have
8 a done **b** drunk **c** flown **d** gone **e** had **f** left **g** run **h** seen **i** spent **j** swum **k** taken
9 a She has/'s lived here for 3 weeks. **b** I have/'ve felt ill since 3 o'clock. **c** They have/'ve studied here for 2 months and they will go home tomorrow. **d** We've had this car for 4 years. **e** You've worked here since 1998.
10

for	since
four days	[10 October/October 10]
a long time	I got up
10 seconds	Christmas
an hour	Tuesday

11 a I've lived here for three weeks. **b** How long have Eric and Erica had a new house? **c** Mitch has studied physics since early last year. **d** They haven't tried dieting for very long. **e** How long has she eaten nuts for breakfast?
12 a She's been in Beijing for three days. **b** They've been in Bolivia since Thursday. **c** I've known Jane for three months. **d** I've had a laptop computer since 1998. **e** I've been divorced for one year. **f** She has studied economics for two years.
13 a has he been in London **b** known George **c** they been in Indonesia **d** has Jane been married **e** long has your uncle lived in Los Angeles **f** How long have you had an old car **g** How long have you been divorced? **h** How long has Pete worked in Honolulu? **i** How long have you known Robin? **j** How long has Louise been a teacher?

Unit 23

1 a I **b** II
2 a past **b** yes **c** no
3 a 've **b** 's **c** been **d** sent **e** has **f** ever
4 a broken **b** won **c** flown **d** gone **e** had **f** met **g** run **h** seen **i** spent **j** swum **k** taken
5 a Have you ever been to Japan? **b** broken

a leg **c** met a famous person **d** always lived in this house **e** spoken with/to a king or queen **f** Have you ever won a lot of money
6 a He's been to Japan. I've been/I haven't been to Japan. **b** He hasn't broken a leg. I've broken/I haven't broken a leg. **c** He hasn't met a famous person. I've/I haven't met a famous person. **d** He's always lived in this house. I've/haven't always lived in this house. **e** He hasn't spoken to/with a king or queen. I've/haven't spoken to/with a king or queen. **f** He's won a lot of money. I've/haven't won a lot of money.
7 a Have you been to Warsaw? **b** We haven't been to Poland. **c** He's been to Portugal. **d** They've gone home.

Unit 24

1 a III **b** I **c** II
2 a Present Perfect Simple **b** Past Simple **c** Past Simple **d** Present Perfect Simple
3 a have **b** has **c** past participle
4 a hasn't **b** has **c** learned **d** 've **e** haven't **f** have **g** ridden
5 a learned **b** studied **c** left **d** went **e** rode **f** ridden **g** got **h** was/were
6 a ✓ **b** ✗ **c** ✓ **d** ✗ **e** ✓ **f** ✗ **g** ✗ **h** ✓ **i** ✓ **j** ✗ **k** ✗ **l** ✓
7 a Have you ever tried Chinese food? **b** I drank my first champagne last month. **c** Has your husband ever visited Russia? **d** When did he go to Russia?
8 a played **b** have you played **c** played **d** didn't like **e** have you seen **f** 've seen **g** went
9 a have you written **b** did you write **c** wrote **d** have you written **e** wrote

Unit 25

1 a II **b** I
2 a Present Perfect Progressive **b** Yes
3 a 35 years ago **b** yes
4 a period **b** a starting time
5 a 've **b** 's **c** has **d** been **e** working **f** since
6 a How long have you been learning English? **b** She's been living in Bangkok since 1988. **c** We've been studying in New York since January.
7 a learning Thai **b** been working in Istanbul **c** Mike and Sally been training for the Boston Marathon **d** has Emma been waiting

for a bus **e** long have my wife and I been talking on the phone **f** How long has Tricia been reading the newspaper?
8

for	since
four days	last summer
a long time	I arrived
ten minutes	1999
three weeks	Monday

9 a for 20 minutes **b** looking for a new house for 2 weeks. **c** been dancing together since last December. **d** have been working with the same company since the summer. **e** Bruce has been writing a letter since 3 o'clock.

Unit 26

1 1960s
2 a the past **b** repeated actions
3 a yes **b** many times **c** no
4 a used **b** didn't **c** use
5 a Charles used to live in Bangkok. **b** Did you use to work for Coca-Cola? **c** They didn't use to drive to work. **d** How many cigarettes did you use to smoke?
6 a She used to smoke a lot. **b** Did he use to smoke? **c** They didn't use to smoke. **d** I used to smoke. **e** We used to smoke all the time.
7 a I used to take it for a walk every day. **b** We used to walk everywhere. **c** We used to go camping in Spain. **d** He used to fly from Heathrow airport. **e** She used to work in a big office. **f** She used to study very hard.
8 a used to eat **b** used to ride **c** didn't use to eat **d** used to be **e** used to live **f** used to play **g** didn't use to read **h** used to drink

Unit 27

1 two
2 a Past Progressive **b** Past Simple **c** 'film' **d** 1 **e** 2 **f** the middle of an action **g** a finished action
3 a was **b** were **c** not **d** n't **e** was **f** were
4 a You were reading when I saw you. **b** I met him when I was shopping in Sydney. **c** When I woke up, the morning was wonderful – the sun was shining. **d** I was reading when you phoned him. **e** You were sleeping when I phoned.
5 a when it hit an iceberg. **b** John Lennon

was walking to his New York apartment. **c** when a gunman shot him. **d** when Neil Armstrong walked on the moon.

6 a A thief was sleeping in a house in Paris when the police arrived. **b** I was running across the road when a car hit me. **c** They were flying to Australia when the plane crashed. **d** We were not listening when the teacher gave the homework. **e** What were you doing when you heard the news about Princess Diana? **f** Was I snoring when you came in? **g** It wasn't raining when I arrived. **h** When I was reading, the phone rang.

7 a was breaking **b** felt **c** had **d** drank **e** was drinking **f** saw **g** started **h** phoned **i** was singing **j** arrived

Unit 28

1 a II **b** I **c** III

2 a prediction **b** prediction **c** prediction **d** decisions made now **e** offer to help

3 a will **b** 'll **c** arrive

4 a I think the train will be late. **b** I'll phone you tomorrow morning, OK? **c** I'll lend you some money. **d** I'll answer it. **e** The weather won't be hot tomorrow.

5 a I'll send **b** I'll go **c** I'll cook **d** I'll help **e** I'll stay **f** I'll drive

6 a be very wet. **b** crash. **c** be strong. **d** win a gold medal. **e** be more tourists in London.

Unit 29

1 none

2 a true **b** true **c** now **d** true **e** true **f** true **g** now **h** true

3 a yes **b** yes **c** yes **d** yes **e** no **f** no

4 a 'd **b** would **c** to

5 a Would you like any orange juice now, sir? **b** Would you like your coffee now, [madam/ ma'am]? **c** I'd like to order steak and [chips/fries], please. **d** Would you like to have the bill, sir? **e** I'd like a beer, please.

6 a Would you like (some) pizza? **b** a cup of coffee **c** like a sandwich **d** you like (some) cheese **e** Would you like (some) cake? **f** Would you like a cigarette?

7 a Would|you|like|to|go|to|the|party? **b** Would|you|like|to|eat|now? **c** Would|you|like|to|go|for|a|walk? **d** Would|

you|like|to|go|with|me|to|the|concert? **e** Would|you|like|to|meet|Diana|and|me|at|the|restaurant?

8 a Would you like to play tennis tomorrow? **b** go dancing **c** to go out with me **d** like to go to the party **e** you like to go for a drive **f** Would you like to go to a concert? **g** Would you like to go out for a drink?

9 a Would you like a coffee? **b** what would you like **c** would you like **d** I like **e** would you like **f** would you like

Unit 30

1 a V **b** IV or III **c** III or IV **d** I **e** II

2 a ask for permission **b** ask for permission **c** request **d** request **e** ask for permission

3 a is for a bigger request **b** is for a small request **c** is for a big request

4 a I **b** if **c** you **d** sure

5 a Can I have your phone number? **b** Is it all right if I send you an e-mail? **c** Could you help me with my homework? **d** Could I leave early, please?

6 a Sorry, it's not working. **b** OK, but when are you going to come home? **c** Of course, here you are. **d** Sure, but it's yesterday's. **e** OK, but I only studied it for one year at school.

7 a Can I use your phone?/Could I use your phone?/[Is it all right if/may] I use your phone? **b** Can I borrow your pen? **c** Could you open the window? **d** [Is it all right if/may] I change the channel? **e** Can I/Could/[Is it all right if/May] I have your address? **f** Can I /Could I speak to Charlie?

Unit 31

1 a II **b** IV **c** III **d** I

2 a true **b** true **c** the present **d** the past

3 a can **b** can't **c** could **d** swim

4 a I can swim. **b** She can speak French. **c** Can you drive? **d** They could not ski. **e** We could read when we were three.

5 a ✗ Cats can see at night. **b** ✓ **c** ✗ Penguins can't fly. **d** ✗ Dogs can't climb trees. **e** ✓ **f** ✗ Kangaroos can jump.

6 a Can Paula play the piano? **b** ride a [motorbike/motorcycle]? **c** Can Paula drive a bus? **d** Can Andy play the piano? **e** Can

Paula ride a [motorbike/motorcycle]? **f** Can Andy drive a bus?

7 a the piano **b** ride a [motorbike/motorcycle] **c** can't drive a bus **d** a [motorbike/motorcycle] **e** play the piano **f** can drive a bus **g** can ride a [motorbike/motorcycle]

8 a couldn't understand **b** couldn't see **c** can have **d** can't hear **e** can see **f** could read

Unit 32

1 a I **b** III **c** II

2 a future **b** possible **c** yes **d** yes **e** a small chance

3 a might **b** fall **c** arrive

4 a The train might be late. **b** It might rain. **c** They might not like the film. **d** Jean might not pass her exam.

5 a It's really late now. **b** I ate too much. **c** It's our day off. **d** There's a great new film [on/playing].

6 a It might rain. **b** It might not rain. **c** TV **d** write a letter **e** might phone/call **f** might not [have/take] a shower **g** might go to the [cinema/movies] **h** They might play tennis. **i** It might not snow.

Unit 33

1 a I **b** II

2 a true **b** true **c** the future

3 a offer **b** suggestion **c** offer **d** suggestion

4 a shall **b** we **c** I **d** go

5 a Shall we go? **b** Shall I open the window? **c** Shall I answer the phone? **d** Shall we leave now?

6 a Shall I answer it? **b** Shall I carry it for you? **c** Shall I make some tea? **d** Shall I pay for the book? **e** Shall I open the window? **f** Shall I drink it? **g** Shall I go to the supermarket?

7 a Shall I call you later? **b** Shall I buy the black jeans? **c** Shall we go to the [cinema/movies]? **d** Shall we go to Tokyo? **e** Shall I take my car? **f** Shall I turn the light on?

Unit 34

1 a II **b** I **c** IV **d** III

2 a true **b** true **c** true **d** true **e** true **f** true

3 a must **b** mustn't **c** go **d** late

4 a You must wait. **b** I mustn't stay. **c** They mustn't go. **d** She must go home. **e** We mustn't eat so much.

5 a You must meet him. **b** I must go shopping. **c** We must be patient. **d** She must go to the post office.

6 a must go **b** must hurry **c** must see **d** mustn't be **e** must phone/call **f** must win **g** mustn't forget **h** must clean **i** must leave **j** mustn't worry

Unit 35

1 a IV **b** I **c** III **d** II

2 a true **b** true **c** another person **d** true **e** past

3 a have **b** don't **c** to **d** wait **e** he **f** has **g** had **h** didn't

4 a She has to leave now. **b** They have to wait. **c** Do we have to wait? **d** He doesn't have to come. **e** We didn't have to get up early. **f** You had to wait three hours. **g** Does she have to go now?

5 a [do/complete] military service **b** wear school uniform **c** work at night **d** go now **e** take a lot of exams

6 a don't have to go **b** had to take **c** has to work **d** have to talk **e** had to answer **f** didn't have to get up **g** don't have to work **h** have to wear

7 a Do you have to wear a school uniform? **b** Did you have to do a lot of homework at your old school? **c** Did your parents have to take you to school? **d** Do most students have to have jobs in your country? **e** Does the university system have to accept all students?

Unit 36

1 a II **b** I **c** VI **d** IV **e** V **f** III

2 a yes **b** yes **c** no **d** yes **e** yes **f** yes **g** no **h** yes

3 a should **b** 'd better **c** eat **d** exercise

4 a You should do exercise. **b** You shouldn't smoke. **c** She'd better see a doctor. **d** He shouldn't eat red meat. **e** Should we leave early? **f** You'd better see a doctor.

5 a You shouldn't **b** You should **c** You should **d** You shouldn't **e** You shouldn't **f** You should

6 a You'd better not arrive late. **b** You'd better not wear jeans. **c** You'd better smile at the interviewer. **d** You'd better ask some questions. **e** You'd better not smoke during the interview.

7 a Should I buy a camera? **b** take a sweater **c** I go by bus **d** Should I take [traveller's cheques/traveler's checks]? **e** Should I go at night?

Unit 37

1 a nurse

2 a Are the hours **b** Are you **c** Was it **d** Was the money **e** Were you **f** Is he **g** Were they unemployed

3 a am **b** was **c** are **d** I **e** they

4 a ✓ **b** ✗ **c** ✗ **d** ✓ **e** ✓ **f** ✗ **g** ✗ **h** ✓

5 a Was I OK last night? **b** Was Jon OK last night? **c** Were Jean and David OK last night? **d** Is Jon OK now? **e** Are Jean and David OK now? **f** Am I OK now? **g** Were we OK last night? **h** Are we OK now?

6 a Is the money good? **b** Are the hours long? **c** Is the work hard? **d** Is there a uniform? **e** Is the work at home? **f** housewife

Unit 38

1 architect

2 a Do **b** Did, work **c** Does, work

3 a Do **b** Does **c** I **d** it **e** work

4 a ✓ **b** ✗ **c** ✗ **d** ✓ **e** ✗ **f** ✓ **g** ✗ **h** ✓

5 a Do Jean and David live in Canada? **b** Did Jean and David live in Canada last year? **c** Does she live in Canada? **d** Did Jon live in Canada last year? **e** Does Jon live in Canada? **f** Did she live in Canada?

6 a Do you earn good money? **b** Do you work long hours? **c** Did you study for the job? **d** Does the job need special equipment? **e** Does the job make you happy? **f** photographer

Unit 39

1 stamps

2 a Stamps **b** My mother **c** From [shops/stores] **d** Because they're valuable **e** By [post/mail] **f** 5 years ago **g** It's Paul's **h** The one from Honduras

3 a where **b** do **c** you **d** play **e** whose **f** was

4 a ✗ **b** ✓ **c** ✗ **d** ✓ **e** ✓ **f** ✗ **g** ✗ **h** ✓ **i** ✗ **j** ✓

5 a Where are they? **b** Where did Pete go?

c When did Pete go? **d** Where does Pete go? **e** Where did they go? **f** When did they go? **6 a** Where does Jerry live? **b** Why does she like animals? **c** What time does she get up (every day)? **d** When did she move into the house? **e** How does she go to work? **f** Who does she meet at the station? **g** Why did she change her job (last year)?

Unit 40

1 a II **b** I

2 object

3 subject

4 a subject **b** object

5 a who **b** broke **c** did

6 a ✓ **b** ✗ **c** ✗ **d** ✓ **e** ✗ **f** ✓ **g** ✓ **h** ✗ **i** ✗ **j** ✓

7 a What does the man like? **b** [Who/Whom] does the man like? **c** Who likes the man? **d** [Who/Whom] did the man shoot? **e** Who shot the man? What did the man shoot?

8 a Who shot George? **b** [Who/Whom] did Fred shoot? **c** [Who/Whom] does Mary love? **d** Who loves Andy?

9 a Who lives here? **b** Who said something? **c** What happened? **d** What did Peter say? **e** What did Jean see? **f** What did Andrew do? **g** Who knows the answer?

Unit 41

1 a I **b** VI **c** IV **d** V **e** II **f** III

2 a Yes **b** Yes

3 a be **b** do **c** modal verb

4 a Are you? **b** Isn't she? **c** Are you? **d** Am I? **e** Are they? **f** Were they? **g** Can she?

5 a I don't smoke. **b** Doesn't she? **c** We smoke. **d** Did they?

6 a ✓ **b** ✗ **c** ✗ **d** ✓ **e** ✗ **f** ✓ **g** ✓ **h** ✗

7 a Are you? **b** Do you? **c** Do you? **d** Are you? **e** Doesn't she? **f** Did she? **g** Don't you? **h** Do they? **i** Can they?

Unit 42

1 d

2 embedded questions

3 embedded question

4 a she / is **b** where / the station / is

5 a she wants **b** she went **c** he wanted **d** they stayed

6 a ✓ b ✗ c ✗ d ✓ e ✓ f ✗ g ✓ h ✗ i ✗ j ✓
7 a where the police station is, please? **b** where the nearest bank is, please? **c** me what time the next bus comes, please? **d** tell me where the museum is, please? **e** you tell me what the time is, please? **f** Can you tell me how far the station is, please?
8 a I don't know where Susan lives. **b** know where Susan lives? **c** remember where Susan is. **d** I know what her job is. **e** I don't know where they went.

Unit 43

1 a II b IV c I d V e III f VI
2 a cooking in general **b** one visit to the U.S.A.

3 Verbs + infinitive	**Verbs + gerund**
'd like	like
hope	love
decide	finish
promise	enjoy
want	stop
	hate

4 a ✓ b ✗ c ✗ d ✓ e ✗ f ✓ g ✓ h ✗ i ✗ j ✓ k ✗ l ✓
5 a to stay **b** to come **c** living **d** to find **e** to find **f** to write **g** thinking **h** to go **i** writing
6 a Would you like to go? **b** Would you like to play? **c** Do you like going **d** Would you like to **e** Do you like going to rock concerts?
7 a to meet **b** reading **c** to do **d** teaching **e** to find

Unit 44

1 no
2 a indefinite article – *a*: first mention; indefinite article – *a*: one (of many) **b** definite article – *the*: superlative adjective; definite article – *the*: only one **c** definite article – *the*: second mention **d** definite article – *the*: only one **e** indefinite article – *a*: one (of many); indefinite article – *a*: jobs
3 a zero article: streets and roads **b** zero article: towns **c** zero article: countries
4 a zero article: meals **b** zero article: common places with prepositions **c** zero article: general meaning **d** zero article: sports and games **e** zero article: academic subjects

5 a definite article: uniqueness/only one **b** definite article: institutions **c** definite article: entertainments **d** definite article: rivers and oceans **e** definite article: plural countries, plural mountains
6 *an* before vowel sounds *a* before consonant sounds
7 a ✓ b ✗ c ✗ d ✓ e ✓ f ✗ g ✓ h ✗ i ✗ j ✓ k ✓ l ✗ m ✗ n ✓
8 a a b a c an d a e a f a g a h an
9 a Cats like fish. **b** from grapes. **c** can't jump **d** go to school. **e** need oil and [petrol/gas]. **f** Fruit is full of vitamins.
10 a the b a c – d the e – f the g an h a i a
11 a – b the c – d –, – e – f – g the, – h – i the j –

Unit 45

1 a II b I c III
2 a people **b** women **c** men **d** children **e** churches **f** houses **g** factories **h** buses **i** [lorries/trucks] **j** cars
3 a weeks **b** -ies, factories **c** -s, boys **d** -es, wishes **e** -es, watches **f** -es, kisses
4 a -es, foxes **b** -ves, loaves **c** -s, videos **d** -es, potatoes
5 a men **b** women **c** children **d** people **e** teeth **f** feet **g** sheep **h** fish **i** mice
6 a buses **b** children **c** sandwiches **d** teachers **e** churches **f** factories **g** boys **h** watches **i** noses **j** cameras **k** leaves **l** mice **m** women
7 a potatoes **b** dishes **c** days **d** matches **e** zoos **f** photos **g** videos **h** children **i** glasses **j** teeth **k** keys

Unit 46

1 a II b I c V d VIII e III f VI g IV h VII
2 a me **b** you **c** him **d** she **e** the black dress **f** the photos **g** them **h** they **i** them **j** us
3 a ✓ b ✗ c ✗ d ✓ e ✓ f ✗ g ✗ h ✓ i ✓ j ✗
4 a him **b** us **c** him **d** it **e** them **f** them **g** me **h** her **i** it **j** you
5 a she **b** him **c** she **d** them **e** they **f** us

Unit 47

1 yes

2 Countable	**Uncountable**
tomatoes	pasta
onions	cheese

mushrooms   salt
oranges   pepper
                   salad
                   lettuce
                   spaghetti
                   wine

3 a true **b** true **c** false **d** negative **e** true **f** negative **g** true **h** false **i** true **j** true
4 a ✓ **b** ✓ **c** ✓ **d** ✓ **e** ✗ **f** ✓ **g** ✓ **h** ✗ **i** ✓ **j** ✗ **k** ✓ **l** ✓ **m** ✓ **n** ✗ **o** ✓ **p** ✓ **q** ✓ **r** ✓ **s** ✓
5 a ✓ **b** ✗ **c** ✗ **d** ✓ **e** ✗ **f** ✓ **g** ✗ **h** ✓ **i** ✓ **j** ✗ **k** ✗ **l** ✓
6 a glass **b** a glass **c** a chocolate **d** chocolate **e** some cake **f** a cake
7 a any **b** some **c** any **d** some **e** any **f** some
8 a a lot of **b** a lot of **c** much/a lot of **d** many/a lot of **e** much/a lot of **f** a lot of/many **g** much/a lot of

Unit 48

1 A
2 a shorter **b** -er, thinner **c** -i-, -er, easier **d** more, more valuable **e** worse, further
3 than
4

+ -r	+ -er	y + ier	more…	double consonant	irregular
nicer	older	easier	more comfortable	hotter	worse
safer	faster	luckier	more boring	wetter	better
					farther or further

5 a ✓ **b** ✗ **c** ✗ **d** ✓ **e** ✓ **f** ✗ **g** ✗ **h** ✓ **i** ✗ **j** ✓ **k** ✗ **l** ✓
6 a The country is cheaper than the city. **b** healthier than the city **c** is more expensive than the country **d** The country is safer than the city. **e** The city is noisier than the country.
7 a Oporto is bigger than Faro. **b** more expensive **c** Faro is smaller than Oporto. **d** Faro is sunnier than Oporto. **e** Faro is hotter than Oporto. **f** Oporto is cooler than Faro. **g** Faro is cheaper than Oporto. **j** Oporto is cloudier than Faro.

Unit 49

1 a Patrick **b** Wendy **c** Anna
2 a his **b** my **c** your **d** her **e** its **f** our **g** their
3 a ✓ **b** ✗ **c** ✓ **d** ✗ **e** ✓ **f** ✗ **g** ✗ **h** ✓ **i** ✗ **j** ✗ **k** ✓ **l** ✗ **m** ✗ **n** ✗ **o** ✓ **p** ✗
4 a her **b** I **c** his **d** my **e** their **f** Peter's **g**

Mary's **h** our **i** she, my
5 a her **b** their **c** its **d** their **e** its

Unit 50

1 True
2 adverbs
3 a -ly, badly **b** -i-, heavily **c** early
4 a quickly **b** badly **c** easy **d** fast **e** hard **f** early **g** late **h** well
5 a She speaks Russian very well. **b** He speaks Thai very fast. **c** The service here is very quick. **d** Mothers work very hard at home. **e** The bus came late. **f** Run quickly – the train is here.
6 a hard **b** easy **c** quietly **d** noisy **e** quickly **f** quick **g** well **h** good **i** good
7 a late, well, hard, slowly, carefully **b** slowly, carefully **c** late, slowly **d** fluently, well, slowly, carefully **e** well
8 a dangerously **b** fast **c** carefully **d** well **e** badly **f** hard **g** angrily

Unit 51

1 a I **b** III **c** II **d** VI **e** VII **f** IV **g** V
2 a on **b** near **c** next to **d** behind **e** opposite **f** in front of **g** on
3 a on **b** next to **c** near **d** in front of **e** opposite **f** on **g** behind
4 a next to **b** opposite **c** on **d** near **e** next to **f** on
5 a next to **b** next to **c** near **d** behind **e** in front of **f** opposite **g** on **h** on

Unit 52

1 a At midnight – which is too late really. **b** Yes! At 5:30 A.M. usually. **c** At Christmas – that's when we all get together. **d** [At/On] the weekend. That's when I see all the new films. **e** At breakfast time with a croissant. **f** On Friday and I was two weeks late!
2 a Yes, my birthday is on Christmas Day! **b** On [17th June/June 17th] – it was a sunny day. **c** That was in 1996. Donovan Bailey won gold in the 100 [metres/meters]. **d** In August – I'm flying to Sydney. **e** In the morning. I feel awake then. **f** In the [autumn/fall] – I'm studying history.
3 a at 5:30 A.M. **b** breakfast time **c** at Christmas **d** at the weekend **e** Friday **f** on

[17th June/June 17th] **g** 1996 **h** in the morning **i** in the [autumn/fall] **j** in August
4 a at **b** on **c** in
5 a Come on Monday. **b** We leave on Thursday. **c** Come on Tuesday morning. **d** I can't sleep at night. **e** Come in the morning. **f** Come next Wednesday.
6 a [at/on] **b** on **c** on **d** at, on **e** on **f** at
7 a – **b** on **c** at **d** in **e** at **f** [at/on] **g** at, on **h** – **i** on **j** At **k** in

Unit 53

1 one
2 a sat down **b** went out **c** got up **d** looked up **e** went in **f** came in
3 a up **b** down **c** out **d** on **e** out **f** up **g** down **h** down **i** in
4 a up **b** in **c** down **d** on **e** down **f** out **g** up **h** down
5 a came **b** went **c** got **d** went **e** go **f** get **g** looked

Unit 54

1 false
2 a sat down **b** went out **c** looked up **d** came in
3 a turned off **b** turned on
4 a the light **b** on **c** it
5 a turned **b** off **c** it off
6 a He put his shoes on. **b** I took the phone and rang up Jean. **c** It was hot so she took off her coat. **d** I dropped my keys and quickly picked them up. **e** She finished the book and put it down. **f** It was a new word so I looked it up in the dictionary. **g** There was no smoking in the office so she put out her cigarette. **h** He made a mistake so he crossed his name out.
7 a correct **b** mistake: put down it → put it down **c** correct
8 a She put the hat on. She put on the hat. She put it on. **b** He [rang/called] up the director. He [rang/called] the director up. He [rang/called] him up. **c** She took off her clothes. She took them off. She took her clothes off **d** He picked up the keys. He picked the keys up. He picked them up.
9 a on **b** on **c** off **d** up **e** off
10 a picked **b** put **c** looked **d** put **e** crossed

Index

Other related titles

BRITISH ENGLISH

Sandra Stevens

If you know some English already and want to learn more without a teacher, this book is for you. *Teach Yourself British English* is easy to use and will give you the confidence to communicate in everyday situations. The course contains:

- clear and simple explanations
- interesting examples and exercises
- lots of practice in communication, grammar, vocabulary and pronunciation
- special sections which answer common questions and help you avoid making mistakes
- revision tests for you to check your progress
- information about British life and customs

Teach Yourself British English will help you to improve quickly and without a teacher.

The best way to learn English is in English!

TEACH YOURSELF

AMERICAN ENGLISH

Sandra Stevens

If you know some English already and want to learn more without a teacher, this book is for you. *Teach Yourself American English* is easy to use and will give you the confidence to communicate in everyday situations. The course contains:

- clear and simple explanations
- interesting examples and exercises
- lots of practice in communication, grammar, vocabulary and pronunciation
- special sections which answer common questions and help you avoid making mistakes
- revision tests for you to check your progress

Teach Yourself American English will help you to improve quickly and without a teacher.

The best way to learn English is in English!